A Williamson *Kids Can!*® Book

Cut-Paper Play!

Dazzling Creations from Construction Paper

A Williamson *Kids Can!*® Book

Cut-Paper Play!

Dazzling Creations from Construction Paper

Sandi Henry

**Illustrations by
Norma Jean Jourdenais**

WILLIAMSON PUBLISHING COMPANY
CHARLOTTE, VERMONT 05445

Dedication

To my favorite art students: my children Jessica, Joseph, Lydia, and Laura.

Acknowledgements

I am thankful to God for giving me a creative mind and the opportunity to use that gift in writing this book. I'm thankful to my husband Terry, for his encouragement and his computer assistance.

A special thank you to my friend Janet Powell, for using her talent in writing the introduction for each art project, and to my children and art students at Appalachian Christian School, for testing the art projects.

I'm grateful for my parents' encouragement and support during the writing of this book. Thanks also to Lee Aldridge, for sharing her art ideas with me.

I wish to thank Williamson Publishing Company for taking a chance with me, a first-time author, and Jennifer Ingersoll for her editorial skill in the revision of the text.

Library of Congress Cataloging-in-Publication Data

Henry, Sandi, 1951-
  Cut-paper play!: dazzling creations from construction paper/ by Sandi Henry.
     p.   cm.
  "A Williamson kids can! book."
  Includes index.
  Summary: Contains instructions for more than eighty two- and three-dimensional construction paper creations, including a Matisse cut-out, a hanging snake mobile, and a personal desktop robot.
    ISBN: 1-885593-05-8 (alk. paper)
    1. Paper work—Juvenile literature.   [1. Paper work. 2. Handicraft.]   I. Title.
TT870.H43 1997
745.54—dc20   96-33183
                                  CIP
                                   AC

Credits

Cover design: TREZZO-BRAREN STUDIO
Interior design: JOSEPH LEE DESIGN, INC.
Illustrations: NORMA JEAN JOURDENAIS
Printing: CAPITAL CITY PRESS

Williamson Publishing Co.
P.O. Box 185
Charlotte, Vermont 05445
1-800-234-8791

Manufactured in the United States of America

10 9 8 7 6 5 4 3 2 1

Notice: The information contained in this book is true, complete, and accurate to the best of our knowledge. All recommendations and suggestions are made without any guarantees on the part of the author or Williamson Publishing. The author and publisher disclaim all liability incurred in connection with the use of this information.

Table of Contents

As Easy as 1, 2, 3!

Paper, paste, and scissors! 1, 2, 3! Colorful construction paper is the perfect medium for anyone who loves making art. Tear, fold, weave, curl, fringe, loop — these techniques offer you as much variety of expression as any artist could want. Add a palette of papers and color and you can transform a sheet of paper into a three-dimensional bird or create a cut-paper still-life in the style of Henri Matisse!

Let the Creativity Flow

There's plenty of room to apply your creative flair to the art experiences in *Cut-Paper Play!* Though directions for some projects may be very specific, don't let what's listed on the page limit your desire to make something entirely different. In most cases, paper sizes are approximate and suggested colors are only meant to serve as a jumping off place for your imagination. In every case, go with what's exciting to you. If a purple monkey sounds more fun than a brown one, make it! Likewise, snowflakes don't have to be white and the sky certainly doesn't have to be blue. Experiment with shading by using darker colors for dramatic effects or by using contrasting colors (see page 111).

Proportion: Proportion means the relationship of one part to another. Thus, if you increase the size of one part of a creation, you would likely want to change the dimensions of related parts so they "fit" together - unless, that is, you intend to make one thing oversized for emphasis or humor.

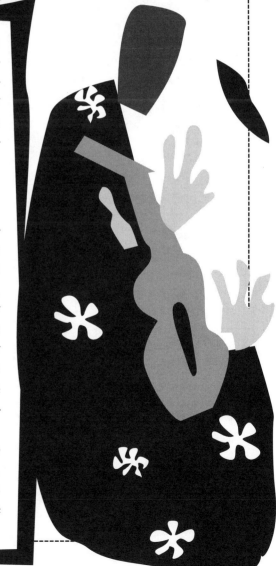

Keys to Confidence

Each art and craft experience has been evaluated according to its level of challenge based on skills needed, number of steps to completion, and time needed to complete projects. Of course, you can alter a project to fit your needs. That's what art is all about. Look for the following symbols when choosing projects.

 Level A good place to begin if you are new at this. Play with colors and basic techniques. Every creative effort is for fun and personal satisfaction. Don't be concerned with what others are doing. Do your own thing.

 Level Projects have a few more steps and sometimes require additional skills. Look at the illustrations for some extra help. You can do it. Improvise whenever you want.

 **Level** Projects require manual dexterity and more steps to completion. These projects should stimulate creativity by introducing techniques you can apply to your original ideas.

See page 156 for projects grouped by approximate skill level.

Tricks of the Trade

There are lots of methods artists use to make things easier. Ahead are a few tips I've learned along the way that will smooth the path for you when creating art with construction paper.

Glue Sponge Sticks

White craft glue is the best adhesive for paper art activities, but using it can get very messy! Using glue sponge sticks is a good way to avoid sticky fingers and will also eliminate glue puddles. Begin by cutting a small sponge lengthwise into six pieces. Pour a small amount of glue into a plate. Hold the damp sponge stick at one end and use the other end to apply glue to the project. Sponges can be washed and reused many times.

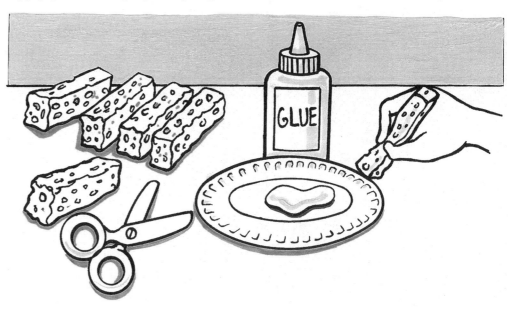

Scrap Box

Keeping a scrap box is a great way to organize and store leftover pieces of construction paper and other paper scraps. A shoe box or any medium-sized box with lid works well. You may want to decorate the box with cut-out construction paper designs, before storing reusable scraps inside. Scrap paper works well for projects that call for small pieces such as mosaics, facial features, and geometric shapes. Tuck away pieces of newspaper, magazine covers, or greeting cards for interesting paper options. Check the scrap box often and be sure to keep its lid closed to keep the paper scraps from fading.

To Cut Paper Strips

Many projects in this book use paper strips. To cut a lot of strips at once, paper cutters (found in schools, copy shops, and libraries) work well. **(Warning: Paper cutters are for grown-up use only. They are very sharp and very dangerous.)** For crisp, clean cuts, use no more than four sheets of construction paper at one time.

If a paper cutter isn't available, strips can be made by drawing straight lines and then cutting with scissors. Or, accordion-fold paper into a fan and then cut along the fold lines for strips. A good time to make paper strips is before dinner when everyone is busy. Sit at the kitchen table with lots of different-colored paper and make a stack of strips for later use.

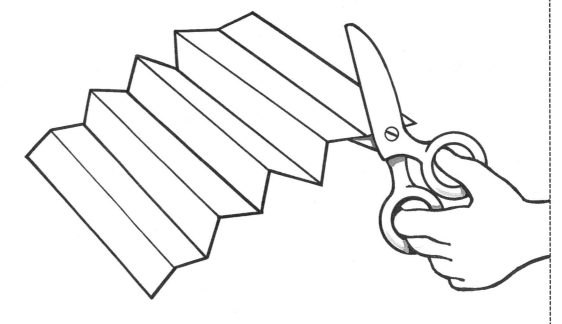

Continued on next page ▶

Circle Patterns

Circle shapes are used in many activities. The easiest way to make circles is by tracing around the outer edge of a round object such as a pie plate, jar lid, or the rim of a drinking glass. Don't be concerned with exact measurements. If the activity asks for a 6" (15 cm) circle and your plate is 6 $\frac{1}{2}$" (16 cm), use it anyway. For tracing, use reusable materials such as yogurt containers or mayonnaise jar lids that can be stored along with the rest of your supplies.

Small: rim of plastic drinking glass, small yogurt container, mayonnaise jar lid

Medium: large yogurt container lid, large glass jar lid

Large: aluminum pie plate

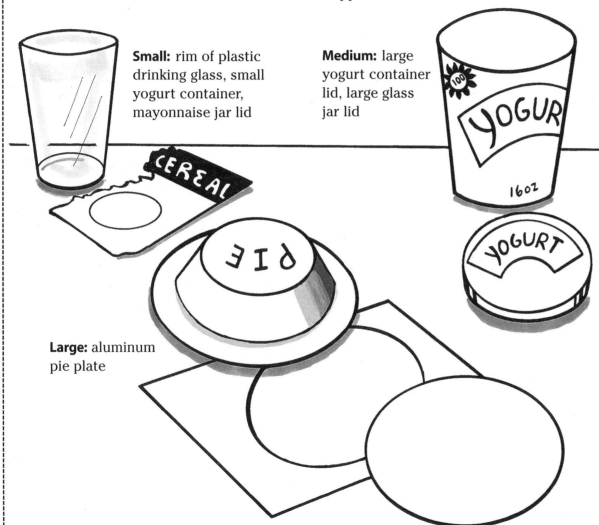

Permanent Templates

Making permanent, reusable circle templates from tag board or cereal box cardboard can save time and resources when creating art. Draw around various circular forms such as yogurt container lids or pie plates (see Circle Patterns); then cut out the shapes. Label each template with its approximate dimensions for easy reference and store with art supplies.

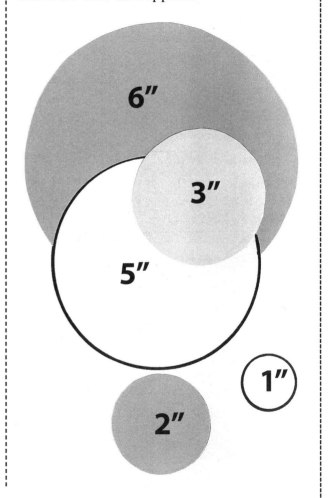

Few Supplies

Supplies needed for most projects can be found in your home or school. Keep scissors, construction paper, glue, paper strips, templates, and paper scraps all together.

⊛ Construction paper is available in one-color packages or in multi-color variety packs in three basic sizes:

9" x 12" (22.5 cm x 30 cm)
12" x 18" (30 cm x 45 cm)
18" x 24" (45 cm x 60 cm)

Keeping a variety pack of 9" x 12" and 12" x 18" paper on hand is a good idea. For smaller-sized pieces, just use a ruler, pencil, and scissors to cut the correct size from a larger piece; then store leftover pieces in your scrap box.

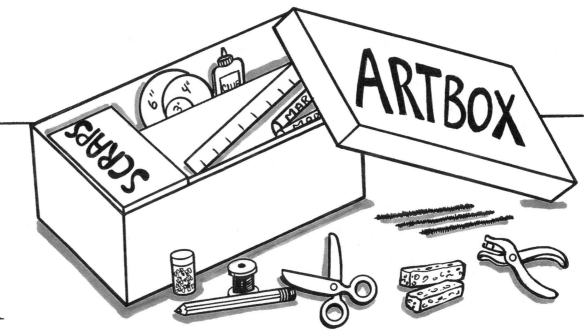

⊛ Scissors and white craft glue are necessary, but you might also use pinking shears, ruler, pencil, stapler, hole punch, monofilament, markers, and glitter. Once in a while, you may discover you're missing the exact art tool or material listed in a project. Don't feel limited—get creative! Often simply stretching your imagination will help you come up with a solution that's right under your nose. For instance, can't find monofila-ment to hang your dazzling bird mobile? Try using heavy-duty thread, fishing line, or string. Having trouble finding a hole punch to make paper confetti? Just tear or cut paper into tiny pieces instead. In most cases, it doesn't matter if the pieces vary in size or if the shapes are perfectly round or square. What matters most is that you bring to each activity the most important artistic tool of all—your imagination!

Continued on next page ▶

Trimmings and other art materials such as ribbon, lace, buttons, cereal, wallpaper scraps, and dried beans can give art an imaginative twist as well as a sense of texture. Try using leftover aluminum foil for a metallic or shiny look or dried grass or cotton to give animals a furry texture. Experiment with ribbons for woven art projects or use newspaper, magazine pages, and gift wrap for paper strip sculptures. But don't just stop there — explore the kitchen cabinets, the sewing basket, your desk drawer, even the great outdoors for fantastic art materials!

Color My World

From the three primary colors — red, yellow, and blue — a virtual rainbow of colors can be made. When two primary colors are mixed together, you end up with a secondary color.

So what happens when you combine a primary color with a secondary color? You end up with intermediate colors such as magenta (red and purple), chartreuse (yellow and green), and turquoise (blue and green).

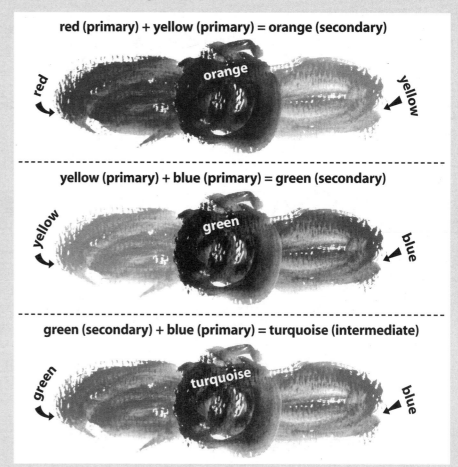

red (primary) + yellow (primary) = orange (secondary)

red · orange · yellow

yellow (primary) + blue (primary) = green (secondary)

yellow · green · blue

green (secondary) + blue (primary) = turquoise (intermediate)

green · turquoise · blue

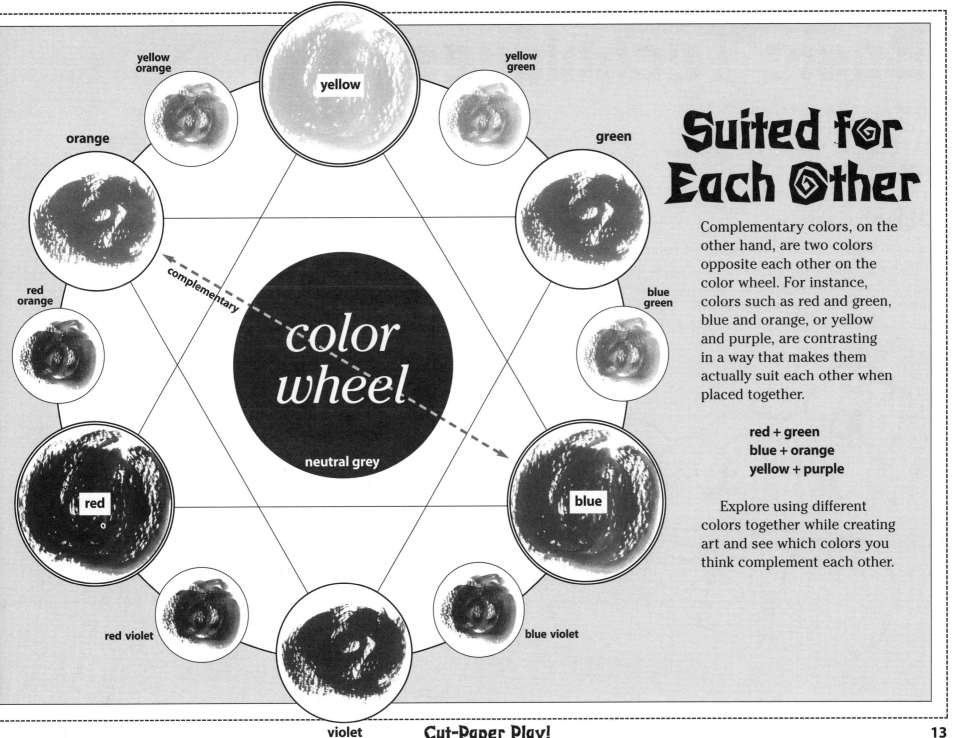

yellow
orange

yellow

yellow
green

orange

green

complementary

red
orange

blue
green

color
wheel

neutral grey

red

blue

red violet

blue violet

violet

Suited for Each Other

Complementary colors, on the other hand, are two colors opposite each other on the color wheel. For instance, colors such as red and green, blue and orange, or yellow and purple, are contrasting in a way that makes them actually suit each other when placed together.

**red + green
blue + orange
yellow + purple**

Explore using different colors together while creating art and see which colors you think complement each other.

Basic Techniques

When working with cut paper, there are a few special techniques that add new dimensions and visual sensations to your art. Use these techniques where they are suggested—and where they aren't.

Paper Loops

Paper loops can be made by gluing the two ends of a paper strip together. They can be teeny tiny and made from delicate strips or big and bold. You can let loops hang freely or they can be individually glued to a background. Loop several paper loops together for a paper chain.

Circle Cone

Make a cone from a circle shape by slitting the circle to the center point and overlapping the ends. The amount of overlap will determine the cone's height and diameter. Glue together.

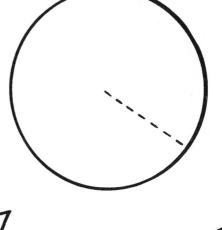

Half-Circle Cone

Find the center point of the straight edge of a half circle. Bend into a cone shape and glue closed.

Snowflake

Fold a circle or square of construction paper in half; then fold in half again. Fold the paper into thirds. While the paper is still folded, cut triangles, half circles, and interesting shapes along the folded edges. Open the snowflake to reveal your design.

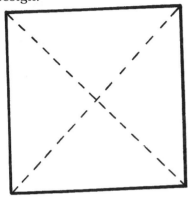

Torn Paper

Torn paper gives a soft, ragged look to projects. Hold paper with the thumb and first finger of both hands placed close together and tear paper slowly. For multi-colored edges, glue together two different-colored paper pieces; then tear into shapes.

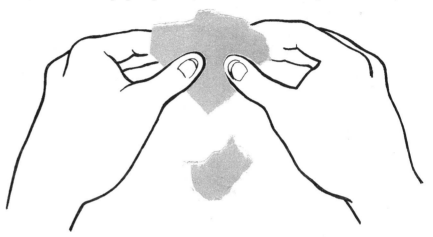

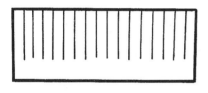

Fringed Paper

Fringed paper works well for design effects such as hair, eyelashes, fur, grass, and flowers. Fringe a paper strip by cutting slits along the long edge towards the opposite side. Cut fringe around a circle for a flower shape, or try curling fringe for a special effect.

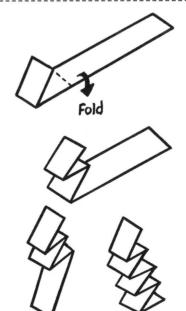

Fold

Folded Spring

Place a paper strip vertically on a table in front of you. Fold a square from the bottom edge of the strip up and over. Flip the strip over and bring the folded end up and over. Repeat the up, over, and flip procedure until the entire strip has been folded.

Continued on next page ▶

Jacob's Ladder-Fold

Glue two different-colored strips of paper at a right angle. Overlap one color over the other so each fold fits snugly against the edge of the preceding strip. Continue folding until all the paper is used. For a longer folded strip, glue another strip to each end of the finished strip. Let the glue dry; then continue folding.

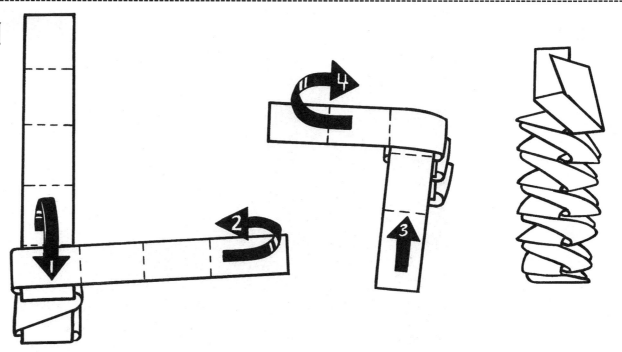

Curled Paper Strips

Curl long paper strips by winding them tightly around a pencil. Remove the pencil and the paper curls will retain their shape.

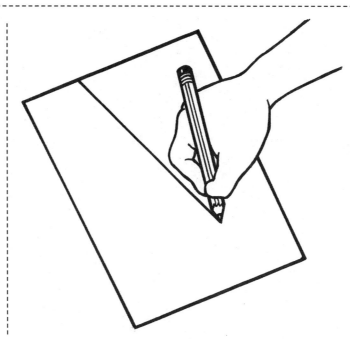

Paper Scoring

Artists score paper to prepare it for accurate folds. Scored paper works especially well for making three-dimensional beaks, noses, and eyes as well as flower petals, leaves, and feathers. To score, use a sharp pencil or the end of a pen with a cap to draw a straight or gently curved line on a piece of paper. Apply heavy pressure to create a groove that will weaken the paper where the line is drawn.

Weaving

Paper weaving adds interesting color, texture, and even dimension to art projects. Fold a piece of construction paper lengthwise into a rectangle. Align a ruler with the top edge of the paper and draw a light line. Draw lines the width of the paper vertically. Cut on the lines and unfold paper for a "frame."

Cut paper strips widthwise from construction paper and weave through the slits of the "frame" in an over and under process, reversing back and forth on every row.

Some variations include cutting straight, curved, or jagged lines or different widths of lines for the frame. You may also wish to vary the strips by using different colors, various sizes, curvy strips, or jagged strips.

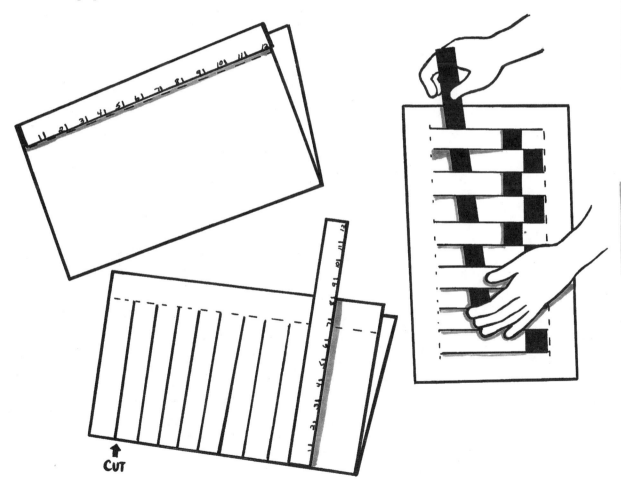

Mosaics

Mosaics are flat designs made by placing small pieces of colored glass tiles, pebbles, beads, or paper close together. Begin a paper mosaic picture by sketching a simple design on a piece of construction paper. Cut or tear small pieces of paper into small uniform sizes and put them into separate color piles. Spread glue on your design, one area at a time and press mosaic pieces into place. Suggest the roundness of an object by going from light to dark, giving the darker pieces the appearance of a shadow.

Brightly-colored mosaic pieces are striking against a black background and dark-colored mosaic pieces stand out sharply on white- or light-colored backgrounds.

Continued on next page ▶

Quilling

Quilling, or paper filigree, is the craft of rolling narrow strips of paper into coils and arranging them into beautiful designs. Quilling can be used to make pictures, cards, holiday ornaments, or to decorate a box or picture frame.

Construction paper strips, about ¼" x 6" (5 mm x 15 cm),

work best for quilling. The easiest way to cut quilling strips is with a paper cutter (always get grown-up help first). Place paper between the ½" (1 cm) guideline for ¼" (5 mm) lengths. If a paper cutter is not available, measure and cut quilling strips with a ruler and scissors.

To make a quill, wind the end of a paper strip tightly

around the middle of a round toothpick. If you have trouble keeping the paper in place, moisten your fingers slightly. Use one hand to turn the toothpick towards you and the other to guide the paper. When you reach the end of the strip, release the coil and let it slip off the end of the toothpick. If you are making a closed coil, dab a spot of glue on the inside

edge to secure it; then pinch it into another shape if necessary.

A small design or picture works well for your first quill project. Make several quills and set them aside before you start gluing them to your background paper. Dip each quill into a shallow pan of glue; then place it on your background paper to create a unique design.

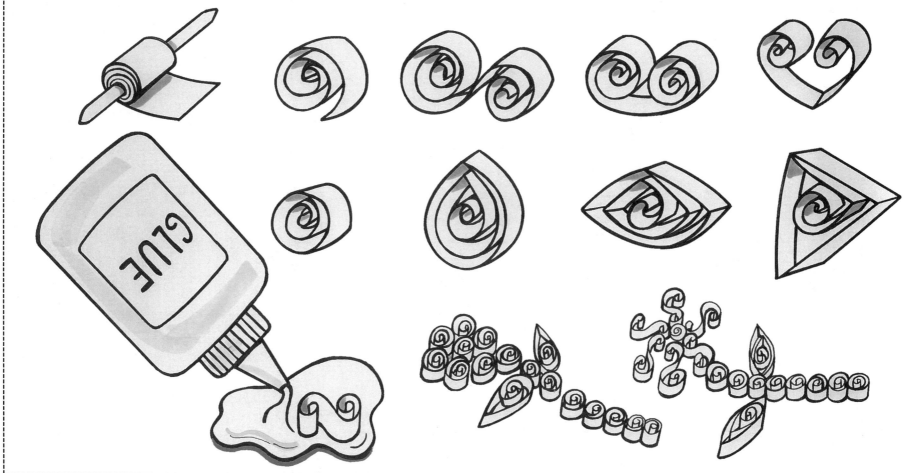

Shapes & Geometric Designs

omething exciting happens when you arrange geometric shapes into repeating designs on paper or put contrasting light and dark colors together—you create incredible optical illusions! Illusions are pictures that trick our eyes into seeing hidden images. Dutch graphic artist M.C. Escher spent much of his life designing optical illusions on paper. Most of his creations were made by repeated light and dark designs that also created a sense of movement or rhythm.

Geometric shapes placed together in various ways can create illusions, too. By using the empty, or negative, space that surrounds a design, you can become an artistic magician.

Inside-Out Design

Making bold, mirrored designs is a wonderful way to learn about negative space, the area that surrounds designs or shapes.

Here's what you need

► Construction paper
   12" x 18" (30 cm x 45 cm),
     light color
   6" x 12" (15 cm x 30 cm),
     dark color
► Scissors
► Glue

Here's what you do

1 Cut shapes from both long edges of the 6" x 12" dark rectangle.

2 Place the cut-out shapes in the center of the 12" x 18" light paper so they are opposite the piece of paper from which they were cut, in a mirror image. Each cut-out shape should contrast the empty space beside it.

3 Glue the cut-out shapes in place on the light paper.

ART OPTIONS!

◎ Try using different colors such as purple on a red background, or green on yellow. Or, instead of a design, cut out your name or a special message to show in positive and negative.

◎ Create an "art quake" by cutting a piece of paper into lots of strange pieces. Glue these pieces together on a larger piece of contrasting color paper, leaving spaces between each piece.

*D*utch graphic artist *M.C. Escher spent his life creating images that flowed together, leaving no open spaces. Most of Escher's designs used contrasting light and dark colors, geometric shapes, and were created to evoke a sense of movement, symmetry, and illusion.*

Fact Find

Puzzling Triangles

Can simple triangles be puzzling? These sure can! The trick here is to place cut-out triangles onto background paper so new triangles are created from the "white" or empty space. Give it some thought and "try some angles" you've never tried before!

Here's what you need

► Construction paper
  9" x 12" (22.5 cm x 30 cm),
    2 complementary colors
► Scissors
► Glue

Here's what you do

1 Cut 12 triangles from one color of construction paper.

2 Arrange the triangles on a complementary color of construction paper starting with the outer edge. The triangles should be placed so another triangle is formed by the background color showing through. Trim the triangles to fit if necessary.

3 Fill in the middle section with cut triangles, forming new triangles from the background paper.

4 Remove one triangle at a time; then glue the back of each triangle onto the paper.

More fun!

Chinese tangrams are picture puzzles made from 7 pieces. Once you break apart a tangram square, you try to make a picture from the pieces. Use a 6" (15 cm) square cut into 7 pieces, as shown. How many different pictures can you make from the pieces?

Try using rectangles or other shapes instead of triangles.

Jigsaw puzzles were first used in 18th-century England to teach people geography. Maps of Europe and various regions of the country were cut into many pieces and were reassembled by students.

Fact Find

Level

Criss-Cross Creation

Lines are all around us—from the lines on the sidewalk to the veins on a leaf to the edge of your bedroom window. Create an interesting line design from colored paper strips.

Here's what you need

▶ Construction paper, various colors plus black or white
▶ Scissors
▶ Glue

Here's what you do

1 Cut several paper strips, about 1/2" x 12" (1 cm x 30 cm), and some others about 1" x 12" (5 cm x 30 cm), from construction paper. Glue 3 same-sized paper strips vertically on black or white paper.

2 Glue 3 of the other size paper strips horizontally on your paper.

3 Glue the rest of the strips in either direction.

4 Cut off the ends of the paper strips that extend beyond the edge.

More fun!

👀

Weave a **Criss-Cross Creation**, using two complementary colors (see page 13). Weave paper strips through several spots of your background paper.

👀

Go to the library and check out a book about the famous Dutch painter, Piet Mondrian. He was famous for his use of horizontal and vertical lines along with color and geometric shapes in his two-dimensional paintings.
Look for his painting *Composition with Red, Blue, and Yellow.*
Then, try making your own Mondrian-style art.

Geometric Jumble

Create an interesting abstract work of art with cut-out geometric shapes.

Here's what you need

► Construction paper
   9" x 12" (22.5 cm x 30 cm),
   black
   9" x 12" (22.5 cm x 30 cm),
   5 various colors
► Scissors
► Glue

Here's what you do

1 Fold each colored piece of construction paper in half the long way. (Do not fold the black paper.)

2 On the fold, cut out squares, rectangles, and triangles of different sizes.

3 While the shape is still folded, cut out the same shape again, only smaller, about 1/2" (1 cm) from the outside edge of the shape. Open each shape.

◎ Make a geometric paper chain. Fold a piece of paper in half; then cut out a triangle on the fold. Cut out a triangle shape in center. Repeat for as many links as you want in your chain. Glue first shape closed. Open the second shape and slip it through the opening at top of the first shape. Refold and glue the bottom of second shape closed. Repeat until chain is as long as you wish.

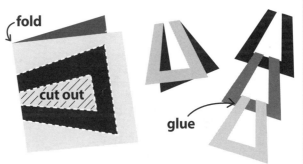

fold

cut out

glue

More fun!

👀
Sponge paint a t-shirt using sponges cut into squares, triangles, circles, or octagons. Dip shapes into plates of different-colored fabric paint; then apply and overlap for random designs.

4 To make shapes interlock, cut through one side of a shape and slip it through another shape.

5 Interlock some shapes and overlap others. Arrange your colors and shapes as you wish before gluing to the black paper.

Squares & Triangles

Squares and triangles are simple shapes, but put them together and wow! The new designs you can create by combining shape, color, and imagination are endless.

Here's what you need

► Construction paper
  9" x 12" (22.5 cm x 30 cm),
    black
  6" x 9" (15 cm x 22.5 cm),
    6 bright and light colors
► Scissors
► Glue

Here's what you do

1 Cut six 2" (5 cm) squares from the 6" x 9" bright-colored paper. Cut some of the squares into triangles by cutting along the diagonal.

2 Cut six 2" squares from the 6" x 9" light-colored paper. Cut some of the squares into triangles.

3 Arrange triangles and squares into interesting shapes and patterns.

4 Glue the designs and patterns onto the black paper.

ART OPTIONS!

◉ Use 3 or 4 colors of squares and triangles for a more colorful design, or add a third shape such as a rectangle or a diamond to your design.

◉ Make shape flash cards for a young friend. Glue shapes on pieces of paper. Or, make sets and play "memory" with your shape cards.

Cursive Design

Cursive hand writing is truly an art form. The style of your signature can paint a picture of your individuality. Use your signature to create your own colorful abstract design.

Here's what you need

► Construction paper
9" x 12" (22.5 cm x 30 cm),
2 contrasting colors
► Scissors
► Glue
► Ruler and pencil

Here's what you do

1 Fold one piece of construction paper in half lengthwise.

2 With the fold at the bottom, write your name in cursive. Make sure your letters are large and have plenty of space between them. Let the letters touch the fold at the bottom. (Just write the top half of the letters f, g, j, p, q, y, and z.)

3 Cut out your name through both halves of paper, leaving a margin around each letter. Do not cut where the letters touch the fold. Unfold the paper.

4 Put glue on the chalk side of the paper and glue onto a contrasting color paper. Display your abstract name *vertically*.

ART OPTIONS!

◎ Make a cursive design for each member in your family. Put clear contact paper on each side of the picture for personalized place mats.

◎ Use large pieces of colored chalk to write your name on your driveway or the sidewalk. Outline each letter with other colors of chalk.

◎ Write your name with a big capital first letter. Look at it and see what animal or plant or object it reminds you of. Then, add a few touches to give your signature some new pizzazz.

Kaleidoscope

Most kaleidoscopes reveal beautiful repeating patterns through a system of several lenses placed above tiny pieces of glass or glitter.

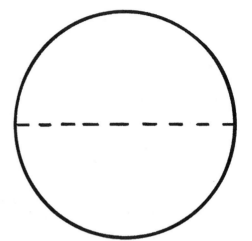

Here's what you need

- ► Construction paper
  9" x 12" (22.5 x 30 cm), white
  Scraps, various colors
- ► Scissors
- ► Glue
- ► Hole punch
- ► Pie plate for tracing

Here's what you do

1 Trace around a pie plate on white paper; cut out.

2 Divide the circle into 8 equal parts by folding the circle in half and then folding the half circle in half again.

3 Fold in half a third time.

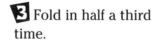

4 Unfold the circle and flatten it out.

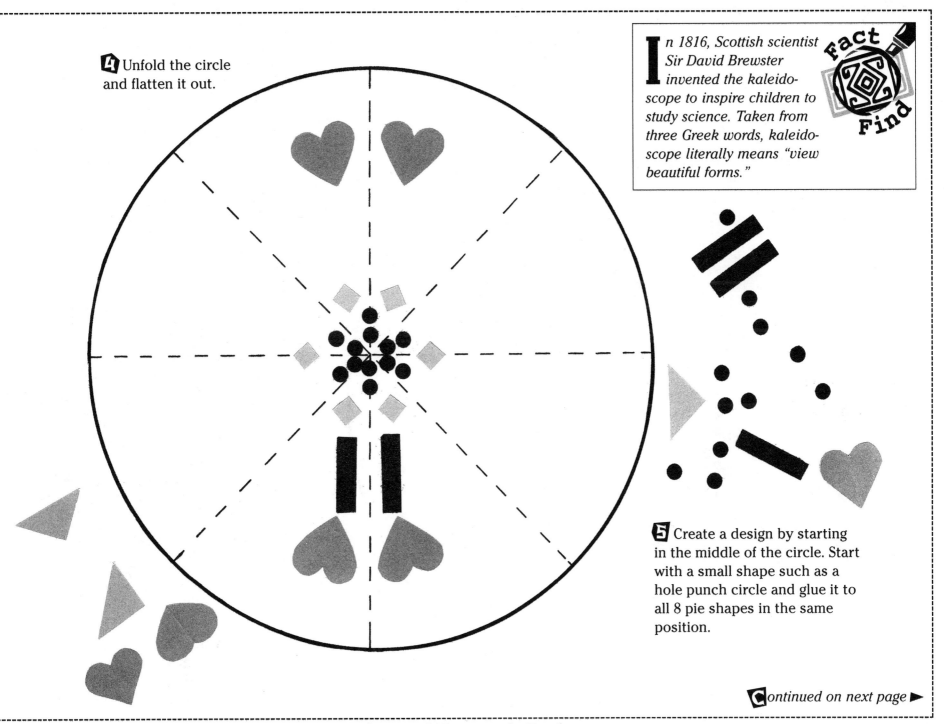

In 1816, Scottish scientist *Sir David Brewster invented the kaleidoscope to inspire children to study science. Taken from three Greek words, kaleidoscope literally means "view beautiful forms."*

Fact Find

5 Create a design by starting in the middle of the circle. Start with a small shape such as a hole punch circle and glue it to all 8 pie shapes in the same position.

Continued on next page ▶

6 Build your design from the inside out using a variety of colors and shapes. Always repeat the same design shape in all 8 pie-shaped areas before moving on to a new color or shape.

More fun!

Instead of using cut-paper designs, try using round sequins and metallic stars and hearts.

Explore M. C. Escher's optical illusion designs in the package M. C. Escher's *Kaleidocycles* (look in book or toy stores).

Three-Dimensional of Creations

What do masks, sculptures, and puppets have in common? Just touch or look at any of these creations for a clue. They take up space in the room and look very realistic, don't they? Three-dimensional art doesn't look like a flat image the way two-dimensional paintings and drawings do. Instead, it has a feeling of depth, which brings it to life in your hands and in your eyes. That's exactly what "Three-Dimensional Creations" focuses on, too — making art come alive!

People the world over have been making 3-D art for hundreds of years so you're in good company. Ancient Egyptians created sculptures, called *bas-relief,* which were raised images sculpted right out of a picture in stone. People and objects in the pictures stand away from the background, creating very realistic images. One of the oldest and most beautiful 3-D paper art forms, *origami,* the Japanese art of paper folding, is still made today.

You'll have a chance to experiment with various art techniques, including origami. Begin with the projects as written, but then add different artistic techniques. Try a variety of methods by adding fringe to your picture, using "Jacob's ladder-fold" to create an object, or concocting a sculpture with folded, scored, and glued paper pieces. Once you get started, you'll find there are endless ways for your 3-D art to take shape.

Paper Strip Sculpture

Abstract art — that is art that only suggests objects, feelings, and scenes through the use of color and shapes — made its debut during the early 20th century with the works of such artists as Russian painter Vassily Kandinsky and Piet Mondrian of Holland.

Here's what you need

► Construction paper
  9" x 12" (22.5 cm x 30 cm), any color
  1" x 12" (2.5 cm x 30 cm) strips, (18), many colors
► Glue

Here's what you do

1 Glue 4 or 5 strips to the paper so they stick out, about 1" (2.5 cm) from the edges.

2 Loop each strip, one at a time, every which way, twisting it like a ribbon and gluing the free end near the center of the paper. Try looping strips under and over other strips for different effects.

ART OPTIONS!

◎ Sculpt a still-life picture with abstract designs from curled paper pieces (see page 16).

◎ Draw a picture of a tree or a lion; then glue down pieces of curled paper pieces for leaves or a mane. For an interesting effect, use shades of a single color or make a pattern with 2 colors.

Three-dimensional art is special for its ability to come alive in the eyes of the beholder. It has depth and doesn't appear as a flat image the way, for instance, a photo does. Most of what we see everyday is in 3-D. Sculptures are the most common form of 3-D art.

Fact Find

Paper Picks

Part of what makes art fun is getting to use varied art materials when creating. Just as you might try using oils, watercolors, acrylics, and tempera when painting, experiment with various weights, colors, and textures of paper when creating cut-paper art.

Most of the projects in *Cut-Paper Play!* list construction paper in the materials, but many other types of paper work just as well. By using different kinds of paper you'll not only add variety to your art creations, you'll become familiar with the textures and uses best suited for certain papers. Most paper materials can be bought at art supply stores in single sheets, making it very easy to experiment with just about any kind you want without wiping out the piggy bank.

◎ For a delicate look, use very thin papers, such as origami paper, tissue paper, rice paper, and colored craft paper.

⚙ For masks and 3-D art creations, watercolor paper, which is heavy and resists ripping, works especially well.

✿ For projects requiring sturdier paper, try construction paper, butcher paper, or French Canson paper.

✸ Around-the-house papers are inexpensive and add pizzazz to most projects. Magazine covers and pages, greeting cards, used gift wrap, brown grocery bags, aluminum foil, and junk mail are great additions to the scrap box (see page 9).

Black Cat

Domestic, or tame, cats are part of a large family of animals called felidae, *also known as felines. There are over 38 different species of feline, starting with the one purring on a chair.*

Here's what you need

► Construction paper
   9" x 12" (22.5 cm x 30 cm), black
   Scraps
► Scissors
► Glue

Here's what you do

1 Fold the black paper in half horizontally to make a rectangle.

2 To form the cat's body and legs, cut away an upside down "U" shape from folded paper. Do not cut on the fold.

3 Cut out a cat's head (a circle with triangle ears) and tail from the leftover black paper and glue to the body.

ART OPTIONS!

◎ Use other colors to make different-colored cats. Cut short pieces of yarn and glue to your cat for fur, whiskers, and a tail.

◎ Create an entire household or barnyard of 3-D animals, such as pigs, cows, or sheep (see Wooly Lamb on page 70).

◎ Cut 5 or 6 vertical slits, about 1" (2.5 cm) apart along the cat's body front; then weave strips of colored scrap paper through the slits for a spotted wild cat.

4 Cut out eyes, nose, and whiskers from scrap paper. Glue them to the cat's head.

Cats can see about six times better than humans at night. Their eyes have a layer of extra reflective cells that absorb light and shine in the dark when caught in a light's glare.

Fact Find

Quilled Snowflake

Nature gives each snowflake its own design. No two snowflakes are exactly alike. You'll find it almost impossible to make two quilled snowflakes alike — but then why would you want to?

Here's what you need

► Construction paper, 9" x 12" (22.5 cm x 30 cm), any light color
► Glue
► Waxed paper
► Monofilament or yarn

Here's what you do

1 Make 20-30 coil quills (see page 18) using light-colored paper strips, about ¹/₄" x 4 ¹/₂" (5 mm x 11 cm).

2 Place the quills on a piece of waxed paper and glue them together in a symmetrical (mirror-image) design, starting from the center.

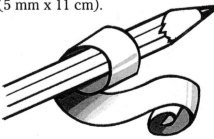

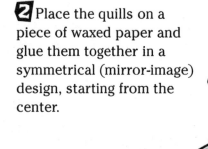

3 Let the snowflake dry on the waxed paper before peeling it off. Hang in the window with a piece of monofilament.

ART OPTIONS!

◎ Make a snowflake necklace by placing quilled snowflakes on waxed paper. Paint one side with clear nail polish. Let dry. Flip over the snowflake and paint the other side. Slip a piece of yarn through one of the holes in the design and tie ends together.

◎ Make quilled snowflakes of different sizes and colors on waxed paper as above. Hang several to make a winter mobile.

◎ Make several snowflakes or other shaped quill designs and use them as holiday ornaments.

◎ Read *Midnight Snowman* by Caroline F. Bauer.

Jacob's Flower

*Visit a toy or hobby store to see a Jacob's ladder, a clatter block toy
that's been used to entertain and "puzzle" kids for over a century. Here's
a variation that can be used in many paper sculpture creations.*

Here's what you need

► Construction paper
  1" x 12" (2.5 cm x 30 cm),
    4 light color and 8 bright
    color
  9" x 12" (22.5 cm x 30 cm),
    any color
  Scraps
► Glue

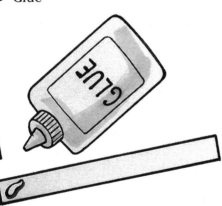

Here's what you do

1 Glue 2 light-colored strips
together, end-to-end. Repeat
with the 2 remaining light-
colored strips.

2 Glue the 2 long light-colored
strips at a right angle. To
"Jacob's ladder-fold," working
from the angle, fold one end
over the adjoining end of the
other; then fold that end back
over the first, until the
strips are folded up com-
pletely. Turn folded strips
into a circle and glue
together for the flower's
center.

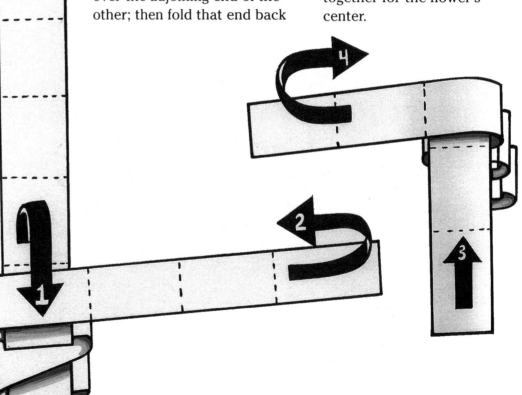

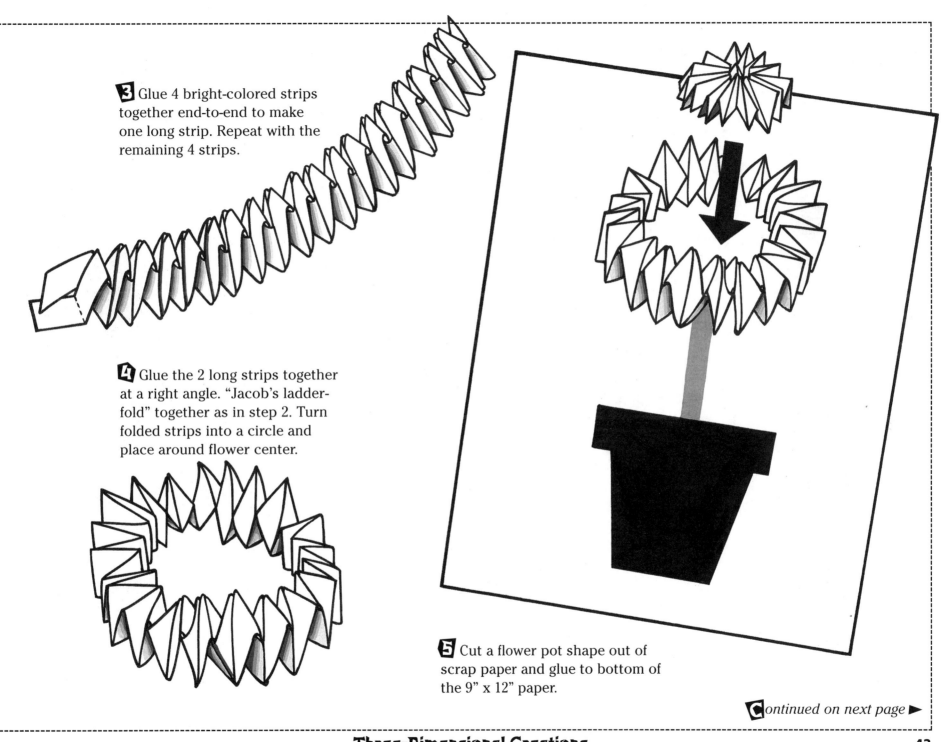

3 Glue 4 bright-colored strips together end-to-end to make one long strip. Repeat with the remaining 4 strips.

4 Glue the 2 long strips together at a right angle. "Jacob's ladder-fold" together as in step 2. Turn folded strips into a circle and place around flower center.

5 Cut a flower pot shape out of scrap paper and glue to bottom of the 9" x 12" paper.

Continued on next page ▶

6 Cut 2 leaves from scrap paper. Score the centers to make them stand out a little. Cut a flower stem and attach leaves. Glue folded flower to the paper, above stem.

ART OPTIONS!

◎ Make a Jacob's Flower with many inside layers. Follow steps 1–4 for the inside of flower; then glue together more strips, Jacob's ladder-fold, and wrap around the smaller inside circles. Make as many layers as you wish.

◎ Follow steps 3 and 4, using ½" x 12" (1 cm x 30 cm) bright-colored strips. Fold into a circle and wear as a bracelet.

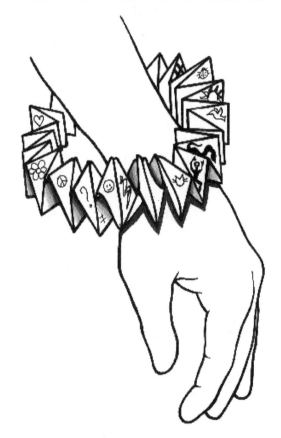

Big Mouth Frog

If you live near water, then you've no doubt heard the trilling and croaking of male frogs and toads in springtime. Why all the racket? Because spring is the time for mating and the call of these creatures is meant to serenade the females. Listen carefully for the common toad, who's high trill seems to carry on for half a minute!

Here's what you need

► Construction paper
   9" x 12" (22.5 cm x 30 cm),
      3 green or brown
      Scraps
► Scissors
► Glue
► Pie plate for tracing

Here's what you do

1 Trace around the pie plate onto 2 pieces of construction paper. Cut out.

2 Fold one circle in half and glue it onto the other circle so that the folded circle forms a big mouth.

3 Cut 2 "U" shapes from scrap paper. Make a tab on the straight edges and glue the tabs to the top of the big mouth near the fold for frog's eyes. Cut out 2 small circles and glue one to the center of each eye.

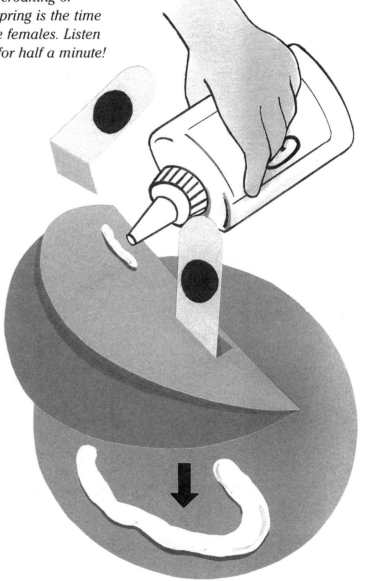

Three-Dimensional Creations

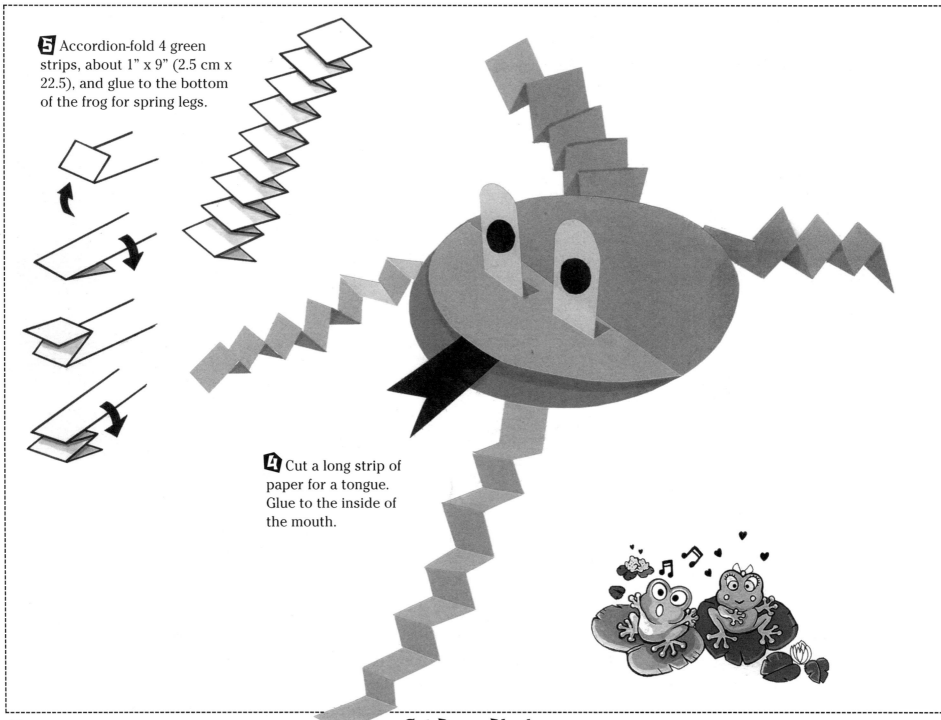

5 Accordion-fold 4 green strips, about 1" x 9" (2.5 cm x 22.5), and glue to the bottom of the frog for spring legs.

4 Cut a long strip of paper for a tongue. Glue to the inside of the mouth.

ART OPTIONS!

◎ Make legs using a "Jacob's ladder-fold" (see page 16).

◎ Make a giant pond mural, complete with lily pads, underwater fish, and plants. Make 2 or 3 paper frogs and display them jumping into the pond or catching flies.

◎ Cut out 4 half ovals from scrap paper for frog feet. Trim around the edges for webbed toes; then glue to each side of the body.

◎ Attach a piece of string through the center of the frog and hang so the accordion feet hang down from the body.

More fun!

👀

Search for frogs and toads in your flower garden and in the damp woods — even by the doorstep where an evening light attracts insects — gulp! Look but don't take home or indoors.

👀

Read *Frog and Toad Are Friends* by Arnold Lobel or *The Wind in the Willows* by Kenneth Graham.

Terrific Turkey

Male turkeys are commonly called "gobblers" or "toms," while females are known as "hens."

Here's what you need

- ► Construction paper
    - 6" x 9" (15 cm x 22.5 cm), brown or other dark color
    - 9" x 12" (22.5 cm x 30 cm), orange or other bright color
    - Scraps
- ► Scissors
- ► Glue
- ► Black marker

2 Fold down one end of a 6" x 1" dark scrap of paper, about 2" (5 cm), to make a head and neck. Cut corners of the folded end at a slant for the beak.

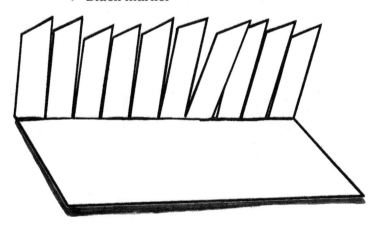

Here's what you do

1 Fold the brown paper in half lengthwise. Make about 10 evenly spaced cuts along one side all the way to the fold. Cut the end of each strip at an angle.

3 Overlap the ends of the uncut edge of paper to form the turkey body and glue.

4 Glue the neck end to the inside of the cone opening.

5 Fan out the tail feathers and glue to the orange paper.

6 Add a beak from scrap paper. Draw eyes, legs, and feet with a black marker.

ART OPTIONS!

◎ Glue your 3-D turkey onto 12" x 18" (30 cm x 45 cm) paper and use markers to create a layered background picture (see page 135).

◎ Glue 3-D turkeys on colorful paper, stiffened with shirt cardboard or tagboard. Tape the top edges of the cardboard together and arrange as a holiday sand-wich board-style centerpiece.

More fun!

Visit a museum or art gallery to see the 3-D works of famous artists such as Pablo Picasso, Alexander Calder, and Auguste Renoir. Or, check out an art book from the library with works from these masters of 3-D art.

Personal Desktop Robot

"Robot," from the Czechoslovakian word for "labor," originated during the 1920s to describe an automated machine.

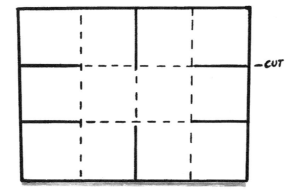

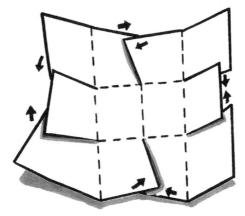

Here's what you do

1 Fold either square of paper into 16 sections by folding it in half and then in half again. Open paper. Fold paper in half the other way; then fold in half again. Cut off the bottom 4 squares.

2 Cut 2 slits into each short side on the fold line, the length of one square. Then cut 1 slit into the center of the long side, on the fold line, the length of one square. Fold

the paper into a box shape, folding the right side into the left side. Repeat with the other piece of paper. Glue the boxes closed and let them dry.

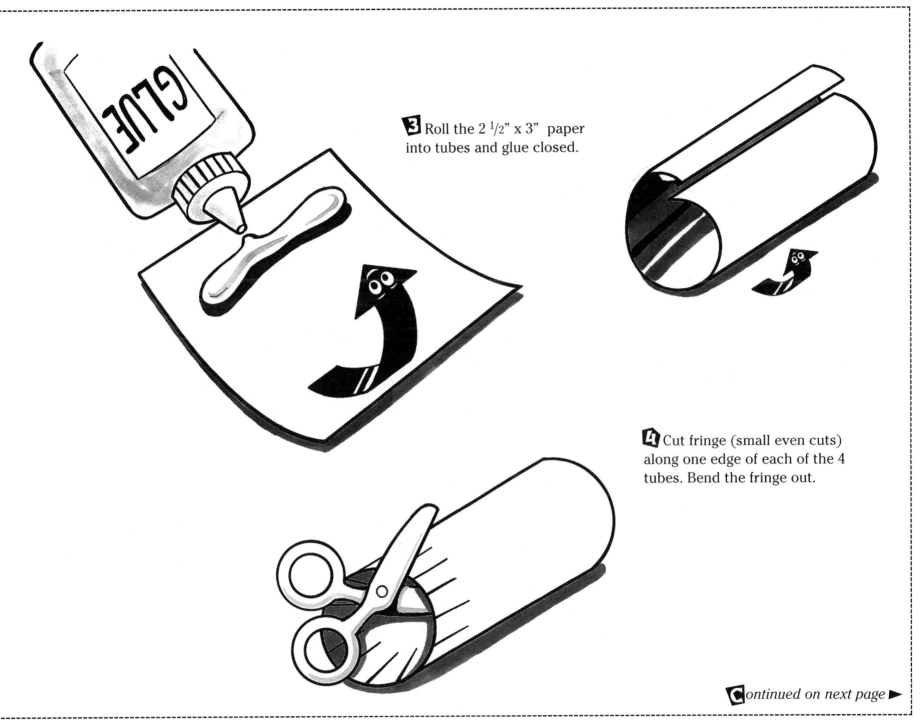

3 Roll the 2 ¹/₂" x 3" paper into tubes and glue closed.

4 Cut fringe (small even cuts) along one edge of each of the 4 tubes. Bend the fringe out.

Continued on next page ▶

5 Glue the fringe end of the tube to the large box body to represent arms and legs.

6 Glue the small box head to the box body. Let dry.

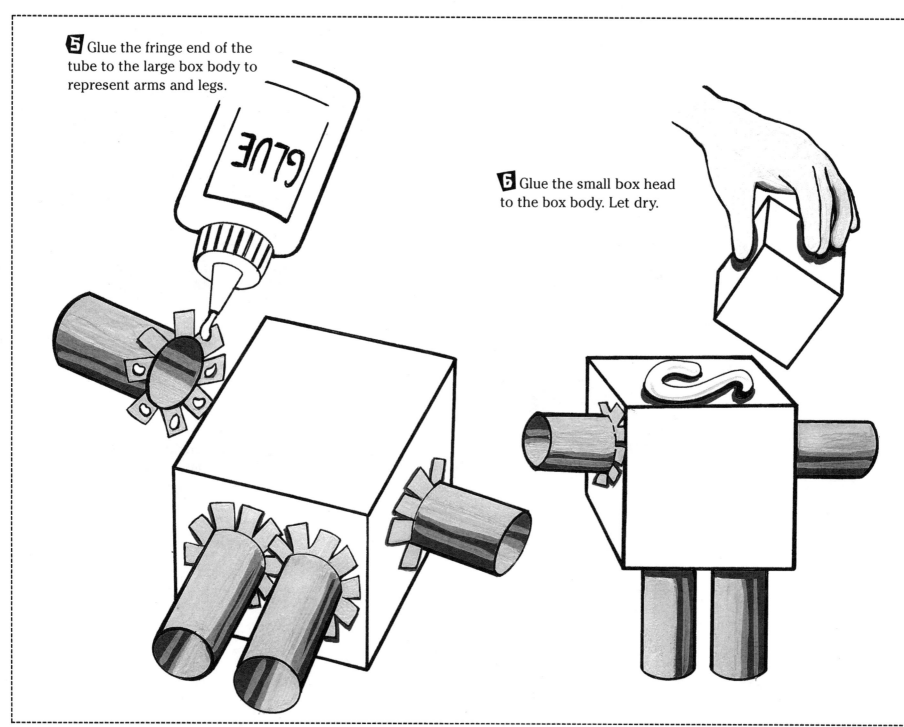

GLUE

7 Cut out eyes, mouth, antennae, gears, and push buttons from scrap paper and glue onto your robot.

ART OPTIONS!

◎ Glue on paper quills (see page 18) for nuts, bolts, and other robot features.

Lacy Heart

Quilling, also called paper filigree, is a craft that was practiced as early as the 13th century. Originally, the paper strips were wound around feather quills, which is how the technique got its name.

Here's what you need

▶ Construction paper
  9" x 12" (22.5 cm x 30 cm),
  any color
  Scraps
▶ Glue
▶ Markers

Here's what you do

1 Fold the piece of paper in half and cut out a half heart shape. Open the heart and flatten it out.

2 Using scrap paper strips, about $1/4$" x $4 1/2$" (5 mm x 11 cm), curl several scroll quills (see page 18).

3 Dip quills into glue and place each into a pleasing pattern.

4 Write a poem or greeting in the center of the heart.

ART OPTIONS!

◎ Glue on sequins and tiny beads in the centers of (or between) the paper curls.

◎ Use quills to cover the top of a box of homemade cookies for a special gift.

◎ Fold a piece of paper in half to make a basic card. Use paper quills to create a design on the front. Write your message inside.

More Fun!

Early quilling works are on display at many museums around the country, including the Metropolitan Museum of Art, and other "big city" museums. Visit one of these museums to see early American crafts.

Yakety-Yak Puppet

In India, crafters create hand puppets from the dried palms of palm trees. The puppets are placed on sticks and twirled between the palms of the hands — lending them the name "palm puppets."

Here's what you need

► Construction paper
   9" x 9" (22.5 cm x 22.5 cm),
      any light color
   4" x 2" (10 cm x 5 cm),
      3 red
   Scraps
► Scissors
► Glue

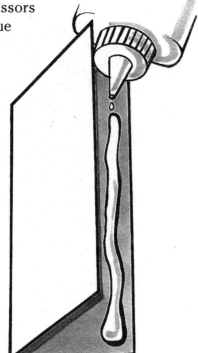

Here's what you do

1 Fold the 9" x 9" paper in half and glue it closed.

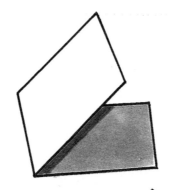

2 Fold the paper over again; then fold each end back to meet the middle fold.

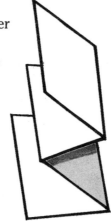

3 Cut out an upper lip, lower lip, and tongue from the red scrap paper. Glue the lips to each end fold of paper to form a set of lips. Glue the tongue to the inside fold.

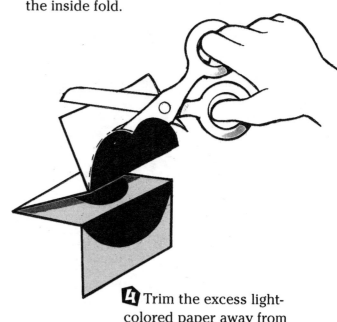

4 Trim the excess light-colored paper away from the red lips.

5 Glue a 1" x 4 ½" (2.5 cm x 11 cm) strip behind the top lip of the mouth puppet to hold your middle three fingers.

Yak   Yak

👀

Make two puppets and carry on a dialogue between them complete with plenty of jokes. Or, give someone special a Yakety-Yak Puppet kiss!

👀

Put on a puppet show. Glue cut-out figures to Popsicle sticks; then set up a lamp or flashlight (at waist level) on a table or chair to shine on a bare wall. Dim the lights in the room and move the puppets in front of the light to cast shadows.

Daffodil

The bulbs of daffodils were used long ago in medicines to treat the sick. Today, oils from these flowers are used to make perfumes. Spritz your cut-paper daffodil with perfume for a lovely springtime scent.

Here's what you need

► Construction paper
  9" x 12" (22.5 cm x 30 cm),
    1 yellow, 1 blue
  9" x 6" (22.5 cm x 15 cm),
    green
  2" x 4" (5 cm x 10 cm),
    yellow
► Scissors
► Glue
► Spray perfume (optional)

Here's what you do

❶ To make the cup of the daffodil, zig-zag cut along one long edge of the yellow strip. Make a ¹/₄" (5 mm) fold along the other long edge of the strip. Cut fringe from the straight edge to the fold. Bend the ends to form a small tube overlapping the ends, and glue the tube closed. Let dry. The fringe should be folded inward.

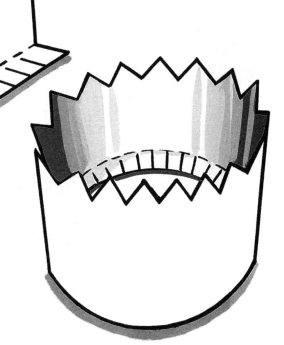

2 Draw 6 ovals for petals; then cut out.

5 Cut a narrow stem and several tall narrow leaves from the green paper; then glue to the blue paper.

3 Glue the petal shapes in a pinwheel pattern to the top $1/3$ of the blue paper.

4 Glue the daffodil cup at the center of the yellow pinwheel.

Continued on next page ▶

6 Spray the daffodil with perfume, if you wish.

More fun!

Look in seed catalogs for different varieties of daffodils to draw or cut out. Draw a vase and add 3 or 4 paper daffodils. Look for daffodils with pink, white, yellow, or orange centers.

You can enjoy a flower bed full of spring "daffies" with just a little planning ahead. In the fall, plant daffodil bulbs in the soil about twice as deep as the bulb is high. Early-bloomer varieties, such as "arctic gold" or "King Alfred," are especially beautiful and will emerge from a cold winter to welcome the neighborhood to spring!

Folded Flowers

O rigami, the fine art of paper folding, has a long history in Japanese art, perhaps originating from the older art of folding cloth. In origami, an artist creates an object by folding a piece of paper without cutting, pasting, or decorating the paper. Try this classic origami flower design.

Trumpet Flower

1 Fold a 6" (15 cm) piece of paper in half.
Fold in half again for a square.

2 Open the paper and fold in half for a triangle.
Fold in half again for a smaller triangle.

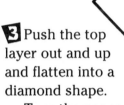
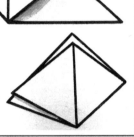

3 Push the top layer out and up and flatten into a diamond shape.
Turn the paper over and repeat for the other side.

4 Fold the edges of the top layer in to meet at the center line.
Turn the paper over and repeat for the other side.

5 Fold the top down (all layers) about a third of the way from the top.

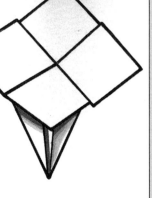

6 Unfold and push the petals down, flattening the two diamond shapes on either side into petals.

Adapted from Williamson Publishing's *Adventures In Art* by Susan Milord

Monkey Business

In some regions of the world, monkeys are treated with great respect. In India, for instance, the people of the Hindu faith believe monkeys are sacred creatures and allow them to roam freely in villages and even in holy temples! This swinging monkey will surely make you laugh!

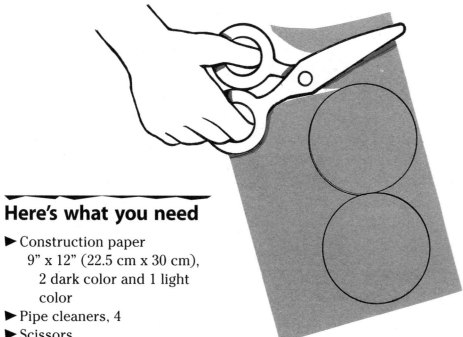

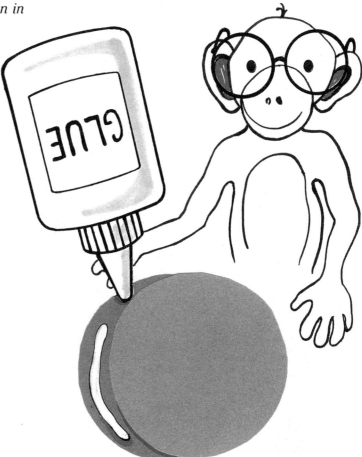

Here's what you need

▶ Construction paper
    9" x 12" (22.5 cm x 30 cm),
    2 dark color and 1 light
    color
▶ Pipe cleaners, 4
▶ Scissors
▶ Glue
▶ Marker, black
▶ Small tree branch
▶ Stapler

Here's what you do

1 Cut out two 3" (7.5 cm) circles from dark paper for the monkey's head. Put aside.

2 Cut out two 4 1/2" (11 cm) circles from dark paper for the monkey's body. Glue the circles together.

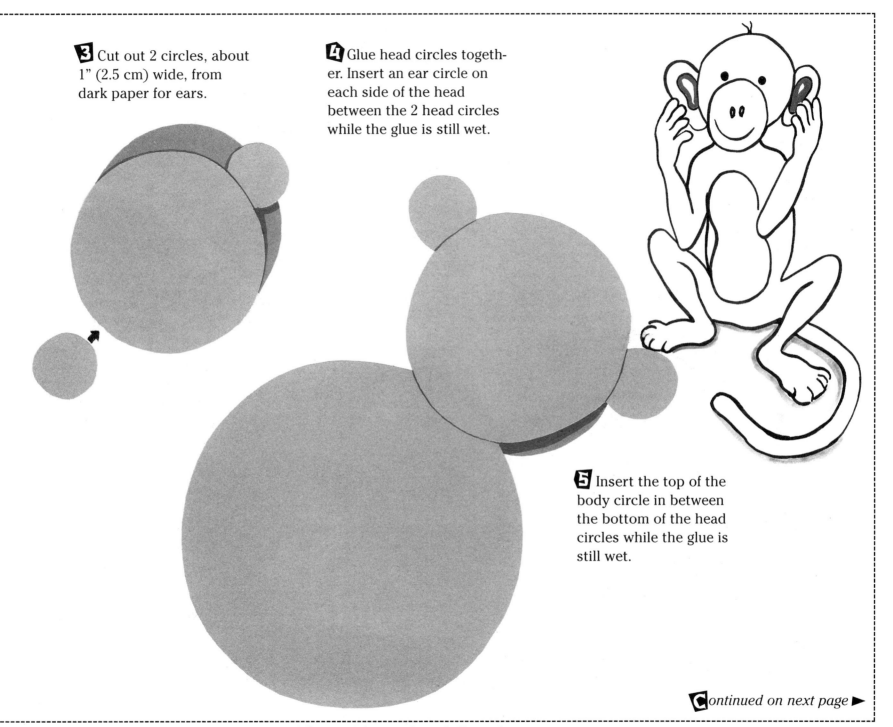

3 Cut out 2 circles, about 1" (2.5 cm) wide, from dark paper for ears.

4 Glue head circles together. Insert an ear circle on each side of the head between the 2 head circles while the glue is still wet.

5 Insert the top of the body circle in between the bottom of the head circles while the glue is still wet.

Continued on next page ▶

6 Cut out a circle, about 1 ¹/₂" (3.5 cm), from light-colored paper and glue onto the dark head circle.

7 Cut out a circle, about 3" (7.5 cm) wide, from light-colored paper, and glue onto the body circle.

8 Draw on eyes, nose, and other facial features.

9 Staple pipe cleaners to the monkey for arms and legs. Wrap one end of the arm around a small tree branch.

ART OPTIONS!

◎ Make a monkey out of dark and light felt instead of construction paper.

◎ Make a twirling monkey by wrapping the ends of the arms around a plastic drinking straw. Hold the straw in your hand and swing the monkey around the straw.

More Fun!

Read *Caps For Sale* by Esphyr Slobodkina or *Curious George* by Hans Augusto Rey.

Loopy Flower

During the 1630s, tulip bulbs in Holland were so prized for their beauty that some varieties sold for as much as $1000 each! Here are some prize-winning flowers that only cost pennies.

Here's what you need

▶ Construction paper
  2" x 9" (5 cm x 12.5 cm),
    6 bright color; 3 green or
    dark color; 1 light color
  Scraps
▶ Stapler
▶ Glue
▶ Scissors
▶ Yarn or monofilament

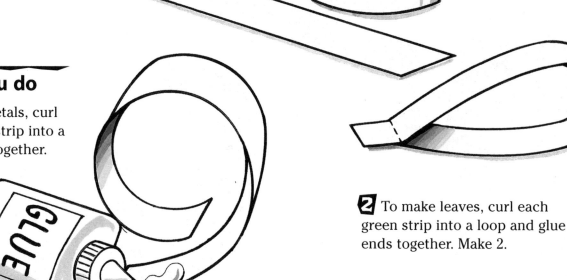

Here's what you do

1 To make flower petals, curl each bright-colored strip into a loop and glue ends together.

2 To make leaves, curl each green strip into a loop and glue ends together. Make 2.

3 Curl the light-colored strip into a loop and glue the ends together for the flower center.

4 Join the flower petals to the center loop by stapling the inside of each petal to the center loop.

Continued on next page ▶

ART OPTIONS!

◎ Make several paper-loop flowers, but leave off the stem and leaves. Connect one flower to the next by making several loops of a paper chain and adding flower heads at random intervals. Hang around your room or along the mantel for an unusual paper chain.

◎ Create other paper flower sculptures by first making several large paper loops; then several smaller loops. Glue the smaller loops inside the larger ones at their bases. Glue to both sides of a strip of paper to form a ribbon-like two-sided flower.

Three-Dimensional Creations

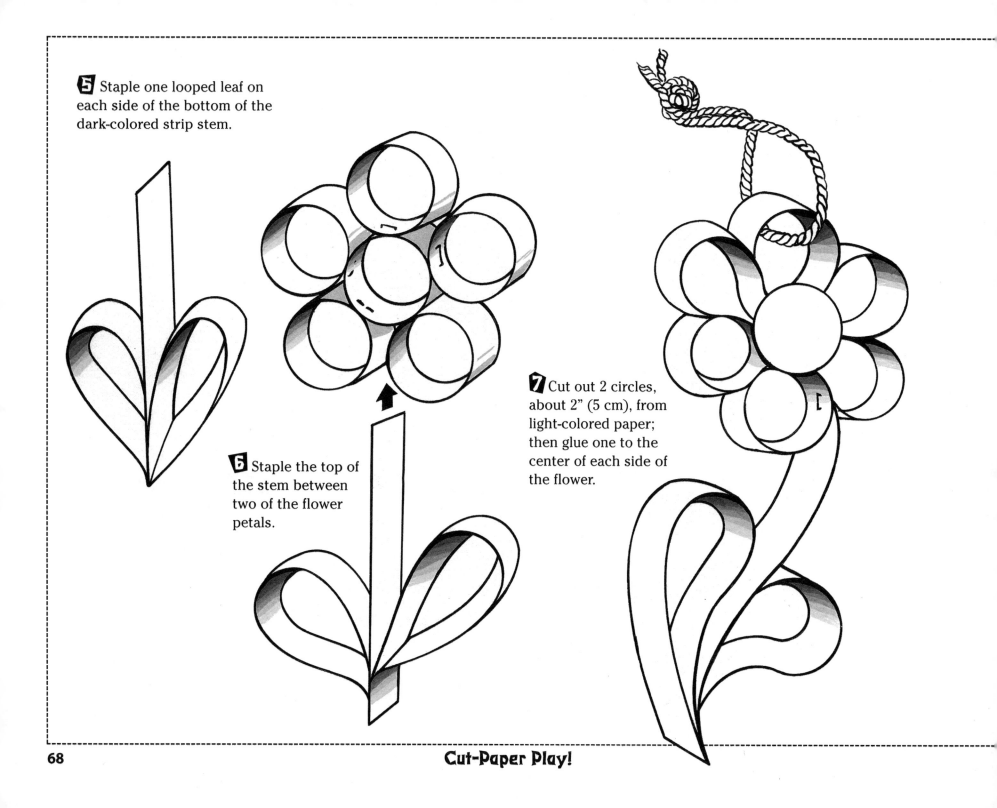

5 Staple one looped leaf on each side of the bottom of the dark-colored strip stem.

6 Staple the top of the stem between two of the flower petals.

7 Cut out 2 circles, about 2" (5 cm), from light-colored paper; then glue one to the center of each side of the flower.

8 Loop a piece of yarn or monofilament around the top petal and hang from the ceiling.

Make your world a prettier place by growing a window box of nasturtiums, petunias, and coreopsis. All they need to thrive are sunshine, moist soil, and your TLC, of course!

Find out the origin of your favorite flowers. You'll no doubt discover that many of them originated in different countries. Do you have potted planters brimming with geraniums? They're native to South Africa. Is your yard or sidewalk bordered with marigolds? They got their start in Mexico.

Wooly Lamb

Australia is the world's leading sheep-raising country with sheep outnumbering people 10 to 1. In New Zealand, there are 20 sheep to every person in the country!

Here's what you need

► Construction paper
   9" x 12" (22.5 cm x 30 cm),
   2 white or light color
   Scraps
► Scissors
► Glue
► Black marker

Here's what you do

1 Fold a piece of light-colored paper in half.
   To make the body and legs, cut out an upside down "U" shape from the middle of the folded paper (do not cut on the fold).

2 Use the leftover paper to make the lamb's head.

3 Cut out long ears from black scrap paper and glue to the sides of the head.

4 Draw on eyes and a nose.

5 Cut out about 20 paper strips, about 1/2" x 3" (1 cm x 7.5 cm), and curl them over a pencil. Glue the curls to the lamb's body and top of head.

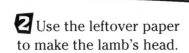

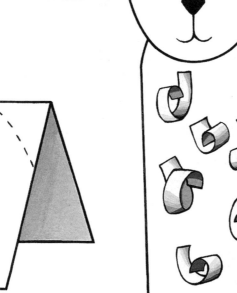

ART OPTIONS!

◎ Instead of using paper curls, glue cotton balls or fabric scraps on the lamb.

Back to the Basics

Many of the objects you include in your art creations have basic forms similar to geometric shapes such as circles, triangles, squares, and ovals.

Drawing animals, trees, or buildings is much easier if you look at each as simply one geometric shape or as a combination of shapes. This will give you a good starting point in cutting out figures for landscapes or other cut-paper art.

Basic Animal Shape

Draw an oval or peanut shape on paper for the body; then use an oval for the head. Draw details around the shape; then cut out.

Trees, Buildings, & Vehicles

Very often shapes seen in nature are very similar to geometric shapes. The same is true of buildings and vehicles. Try creating these objects in your art by using a variety of geometric outlines; then add details to make them realistic.

Create-a-Mask

Masks allow us to be someone else or something else. Use paper techniques such as curling, fringing, cutting, and scoring to make any face you please.

Here's what you need

► Construction paper
9" x 12" (22.5 cm x 30 cm), any color
Scraps
► Scissors
► Glue
► Tongue depressor or Popsicle stick

Here's what you do

1 Fold the paper in half; then cut 2 half-oval eye holes along the fold. Open the paper and flatten it out.

2 Cut out a nose or beak from scrap paper. Score it before gluing it in place. Cut out a mouth from scrap paper and glue in place.

3 Shape the chin and top of head with scissors.

Make an African wall mask in the same way you made the paper mask, only use a square of aluminum foil instead. Press in designs using a toothpick; then tape to background paper.

T he word "hypocrite" comes from the Greek word for actor, hypocrites. *In ancient Greece, it was the custom for actors to wear masks, so they were nicknamed "two-faced." Can you see where our modern meaning of hypocrite came from?*

Fact Find

4 Cut out other details from scrap paper such as hair, fur, ears, earrings, hat, or alien antennae. Use different three-dimensional paper techniques such as fringing, scoring, tearing, folding, and curling to make your mask.

5 Glue a tongue depressor to one edge of the mask and hold in front of your face.

Dog Puppet

Hand puppets were first used in the 1600s by traveling puppeteers who entertained villagers and royalty throughout Europe. Most of these puppets were carved from wood and were dressed in beautiful clothes.

Here's what you need

► Construction paper
  9" x 18" (22.5 cm x 45 cm),
    any color
  3" x 5" (7.5 cm x 12.5 cm),
    2 of any color
  Scraps
► Scissors
► Glue

Here's what you do

1 Fold the 9" x 18" paper into thirds lengthwise. Flip over the paper and fold in half.

2 Fold the bottom edge back to meet the fold; then fold top edge back to meet fold.

3 Cut both pieces of 3" x 5" brown paper at the same time into dog ears. Glue ears to the side of the head.

4 From scrap, cut out a tongue, about 2" x 3" (5 cm x 7.5 cm), to glue inside the mouth, and cut 2 circles for eyes. Cut 2 smaller circles for eyeballs.

5 Place your fingers into the top slot of paper and your thumb into the bottom slot and make your puppet bark.

NEXT SHOW 2:00

More fun!

Ask your family and friends to show you how to make shadow "puppets" on a ceiling or wall in the dark.

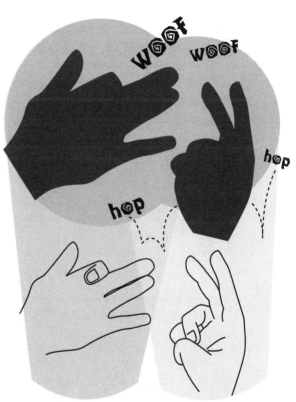

WOOF WOOF

hop hop

Read *Pinocchio* and learn about the world's most famous puppet, or marionette!

Level

Baby Birds

Birds build a variety of nests. The smallest nests usually have the greatest variety of materials used to construct them. Some birds, such as the house martin and swallow, build their nests from mud; other small birds use animal fur or hair, grass, string, feathers, even lichen from trees and rocks. This nest is woven from paper — by you!

Here's what you need

► Construction paper
    4" x 6" (10 cm x 15 cm),
      brown
    9" x 12" (22.5 cm x 30 cm),
      1 dark color and
      1 bright color
    Scraps
► Scissors
► Glue

Here's what you do

1 Draw a long branch out of dark-colored paper and cut out. Glue the branch across the width of the bright-colored paper.

2 Round the bottom of the brown paper to make a nest shape.

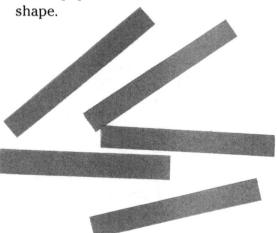

3 Make 8 or 9 slits from the straight side of the nest to about $1/2$" (1 cm) of the rounded end.

4 Cut five $1/2$" (1 cm) strips out of leftover dark-colored paper, and weave them into the nest, going over and under each slit. Bend the ends of the woven strips around to the back of the nest and glue.

Continued on next page ▶

5 Fringe the top ends of the nest and curl forward for a 3-D effect.

6 Cut 3 yellow strips, about 2" x 3" (5 cm x 7.5 cm), from scrap paper and round the top of each end to make baby bird heads. Glue straight end to the back of the nest so that the heads are visible from the front; then glue nest to branch.

Cut-Paper Play!

7 Cut a diamond-shaped beak and 2 eyes for each bird. Fold each beak at the center, and glue the eyes to each bird.

8 Tear and glue a few green paper pieces to the end of the branch for leaves.

ART OPTIONS!

◎ Make a paper "parent" bird with a yarn worm in its mouth, ready to feed the hungry baby birds.

◎ Weave together two magazine pictures of birds. Use one picture as the "loom"; then cut the other picture into strips and weave through the slits for a funny woven picture.

Curled Snail

What could a snail and an octopus possibly have in common? They're both mollusks, a group of soft-bodied animals with hard shells. Although snails are known for moving very slowly, you can make this snail as quick as a wink!

Here's what you need

► Construction paper
   1" x 18" (2.5 cm x 45 cm),
      any color
   Scraps
► Pencil
► Glue
► Hole punch

Here's what you do

1 Curl the strip around the end of a pencil, leaving the last few inches of the strip uncurled.

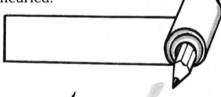

2 Loop back the uncurled end to form a head. Glue closed.

3 Cut antennae from thin strips of colored paper and glue them to the head.

4 Hole punch 2 circles and glue to the head for eyes.

ART OPTIONS!

◎ Make a caterpillar or snake by curling 5 or 6 long strips around a pencil, one at a time. Glue the spiral shapes together in a row. Add paper punch eyes.

More fun!

👀

Send a friend "snail mail." Write a message on the long paper strip before you roll it around a pencil to form the snail's body, then deliver to a friend.

👀

Snails may be small and slow, but they are relatively easy to find in damp places. Place a clay flowerpot upside down, with one side propped up, in the garden, on the lawn, or in the woods. Leave overnight; then check in the morning for visitors. How many do you find?

Marvelous Mobiles

I f you like sculpting or creating other 3-D art, then mobiles are sure to delight you. Mobiles are really hanging sculptures, which can be suspended just about anywhere from just about anything. The Chinese may have inspired the first mobiles with their beautiful wind chimes that create a tinkling sound with the breeze. During the 1930s, however, American artist Alexander Calder turned his fascination with Chinese wind chimes into hanging wire sculptures or mobile (moving) art. Since then, everyone from artists to babies have been enjoying mobiles.

You can create mobiles on broad themes or specific interests: nature, leaves, a favorite holiday, sports, your hobbies. Some great mobiles use different art techniques to illustrate one theme. For instance, you might hang a mosaic butterfly, tissue-paper butterfly, and 3-D butterfly from the same mobile. Some mobiles make the same item — say a sheep — in varied colors or sizes. The activities in "Marvelous Mobiles" give instructions for creating a single object. From there it is up to you to decide how to create your mobile and then what to suspend from it.

Hanging It Up

There are many styles you can use when creating mobiles; some will work better than others depending upon the project. Try these styles or create something entirely new.

Spiral Mobile

1 Cut a 12" (30 cm) circle out of poster board or use a large yogurt container.

2 Poke holes every inch (2.5 cm) or so around the rim of the circle and tie four pieces of string or monofilament at opposite ends and hang.

3 Attach each paper shape from string, with one at each of the 12 holes. Hang the first shape an inch (2.5 cm) from the top; the second 2" (5 cm) below the first; the third 2" (5 cm) below the second, and so on until all shapes are hung in a spiral.

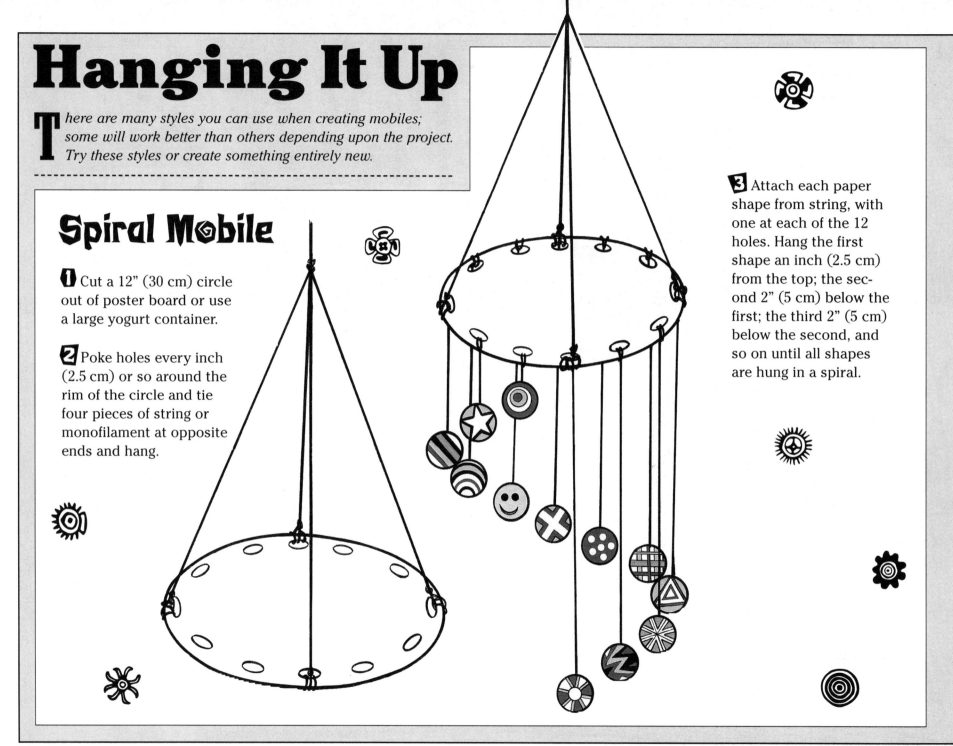

3-Tiered Mobile

1 Find a sturdy branch for the main support of your mobile. Tie a piece of string or monofilament to the branch's center and hang in a low place.

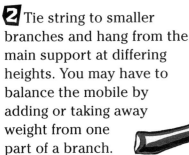

2 Tie string to smaller branches and hang from the main support at differing heights. You may have to balance the mobile by adding or taking away weight from one part of a branch.

3 Use smaller branches or long drinking straws for the lower tiers of your mobile. Hang objects from the various tiers, balancing each tier with an object as you go.

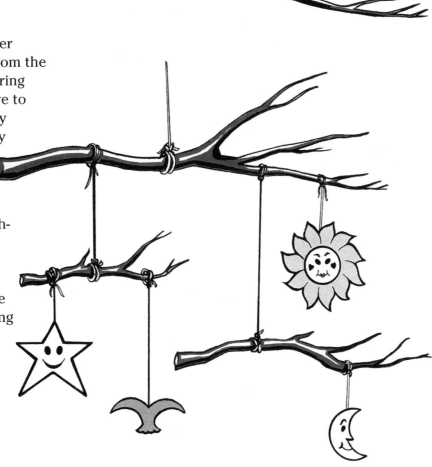

Coat Hanger Support

1 Hang 2 or 3 objects from the center and two ends of a coat hanger. Use various lengths and a variety of objects for unusual effects.

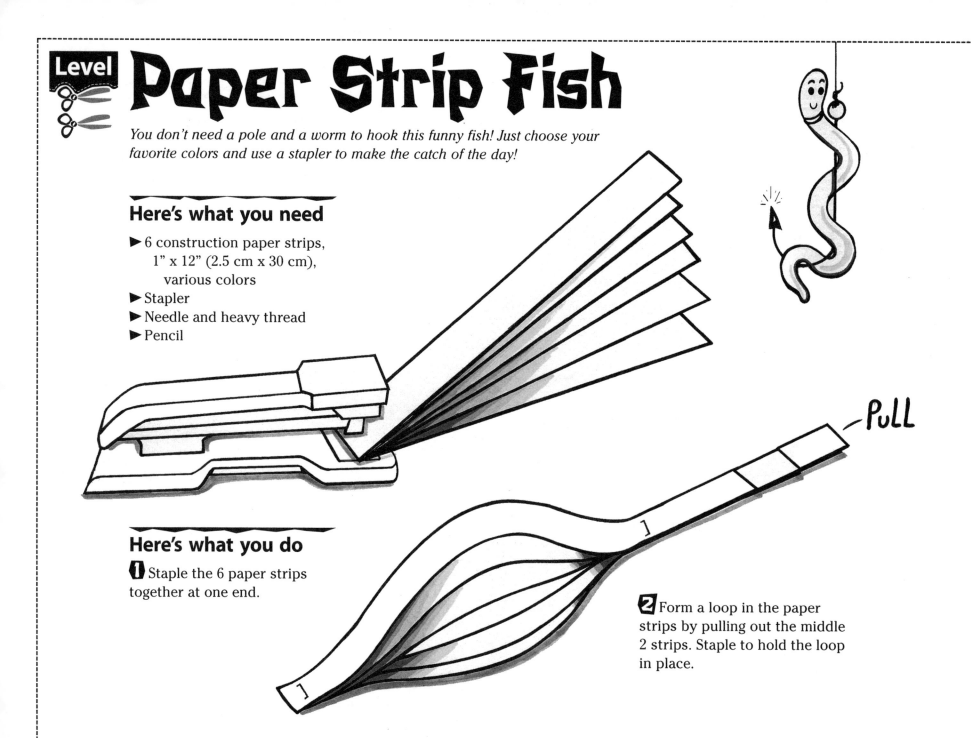

Paper Strip Fish

You don't need a pole and a worm to hook this funny fish! Just choose your favorite colors and use a stapler to make the catch of the day!

Here's what you need

► 6 construction paper strips, 1" x 12" (2.5 cm x 30 cm), various colors
► Stapler
► Needle and heavy thread
► Pencil

Here's what you do

1 Staple the 6 paper strips together at one end.

Pull

2 Form a loop in the paper strips by pulling out the middle 2 strips. Staple to hold the loop in place.

3 To form a curled tail, curl the end of each strip over the pencil.

4 To hang, sew one big stitch in the middle of the top strip of the fish's body. Tie thread ends together.

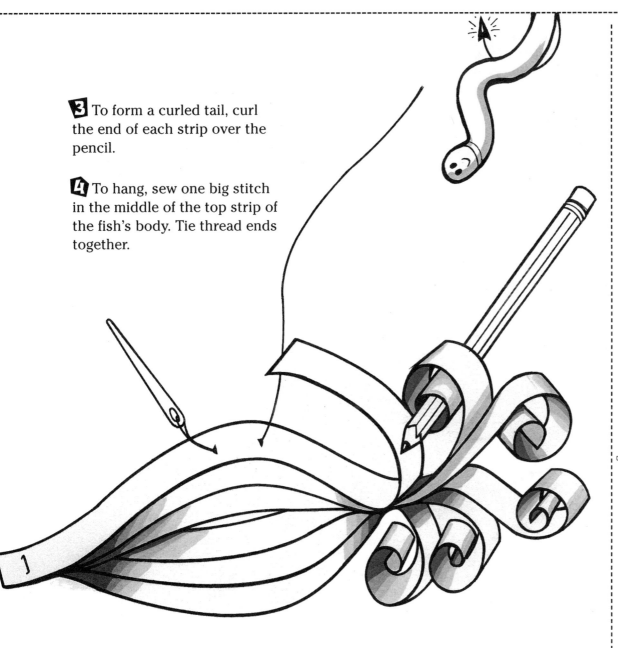

◎ Make a mural of an underwater scene. Glue on paper scraps for seaweed and coral. Glue on seashells or pasta shells. Glue outside edge of body to mural for a 3-D effect.

◎ Visit an aquarium or pet store to learn about fish up close.

◎ Attach a safety pin to each fish. Fashion a fishing pole from a stick and string. Add a magnet as a hook, and go fishing!

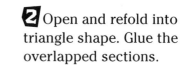

Triangle Star

Stars are masses of burning gas brightly lighting up the night sky. The sun is, of course, the most famous star we see from Earth—it's an amazing 93 million miles away, which is quite close by astronomical standards!

Here's what you need

► Construction paper
   1" x 12" (2.5 cm x 30 cm),
   12 of any color
► Glue
► Monofilament or fishing line

Here's what you do

1 Fold each paper strip into fourths.

2 Open and refold into triangle shape. Glue the overlapped sections.

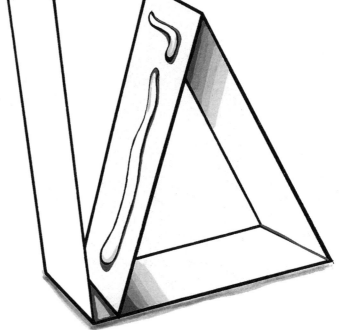

Cut-Paper Play!

3 Arrange the shapes on a table to form a star with six points. Glue the sides where the triangles meet.

4 Repeat to make stars in different colors and sizes. Hang stars with monofilament at different lengths.

More Fun!

👀

Use different-colored triangles to make a single star. Or glue glitter to the outside paper strips to make your star sparkle.

👀

Clear nights are the perfect time for stargazing. Take along a flashlight (cover the lens with red cellophane) and a star chart; then look for the Big Dipper, Polaris (the North Star), and the Little Dipper.

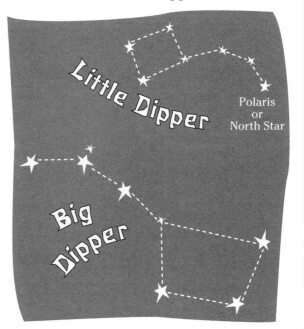

👀

Visit a museum or planetarium and watch a solar system show.

Dazzling Bird

Robins, blue jays, and red cardinals delight us daily with their beauty, but have you ever seen a bird of paradise? This bird, along with jewel-colored peacocks, colorful parrots, and long-feathered pheasants, is one of the world's most dazzling birds.

Here's what you need

▶ Construction paper
  9" x 12" (22.5 cm x 30 cm),
    4 different colors
  12" x 18" (30 cm x 45 cm),
    any color
  2" x 6" (5 cm x 15 cm),
    any color
  Scraps
▶ Scissors
▶ Glue
▶ Stapler
▶ Darning needle
▶ Heavy-duty thread or
  monofilament
▶ Hot glue gun (for grown-up
  use only)

Here's what you do

1 Draw a half-circle shape on the 9" x 12" paper (head) and the 12" x 18" paper (body). Cut out the half circles.

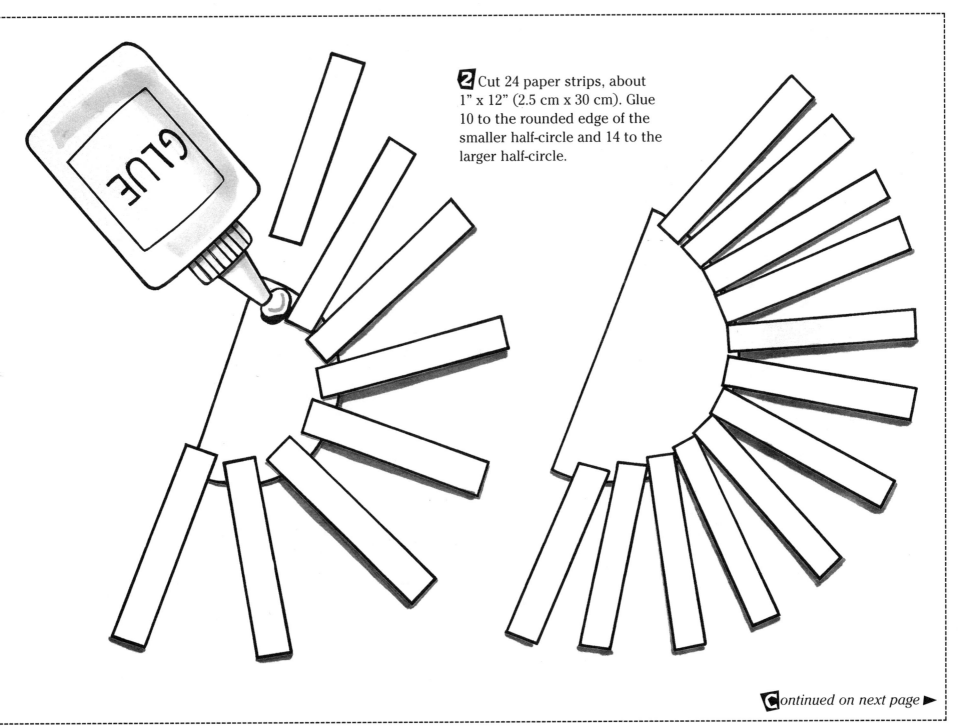

2 Cut 24 paper strips, about 1" x 12" (2.5 cm x 30 cm). Glue 10 to the rounded edge of the smaller half-circle and 14 to the larger half-circle.

Continued on next page ▶

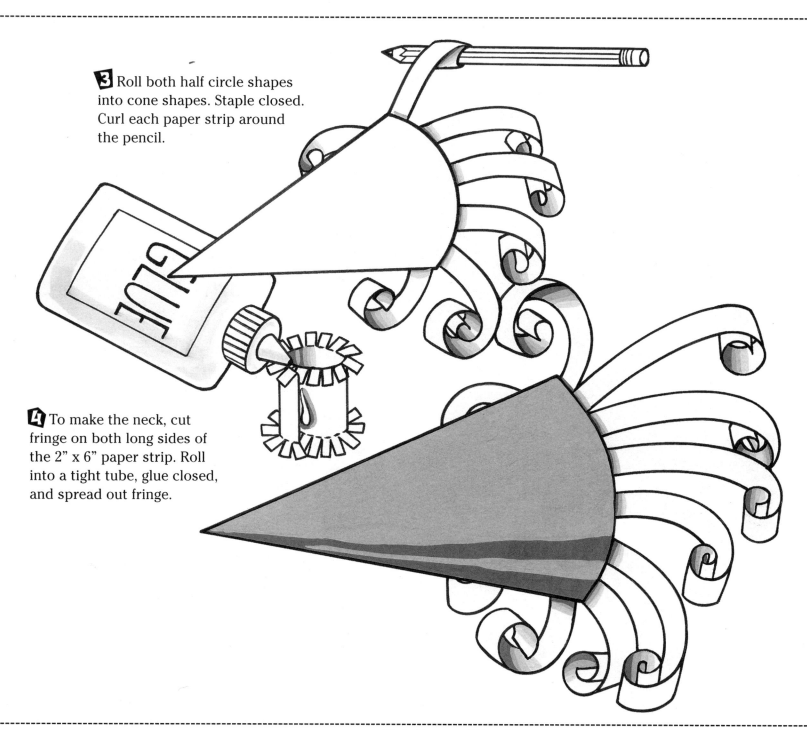

3 Roll both half circle shapes into cone shapes. Staple closed. Curl each paper strip around the pencil.

4 To make the neck, cut fringe on both long sides of the 2" x 6" paper strip. Roll into a tight tube, glue closed, and spread out fringe.

5 Ask a grown-up to help you glue the neck to the head and body with hot glue.

6 Cut out and glue on eyes, wings, and feathers from scrap paper.

7 Make one big stitch in the bird's head by pushing the needle through the top of the head cone to the inside and back out. Tie the two ends together and hang.

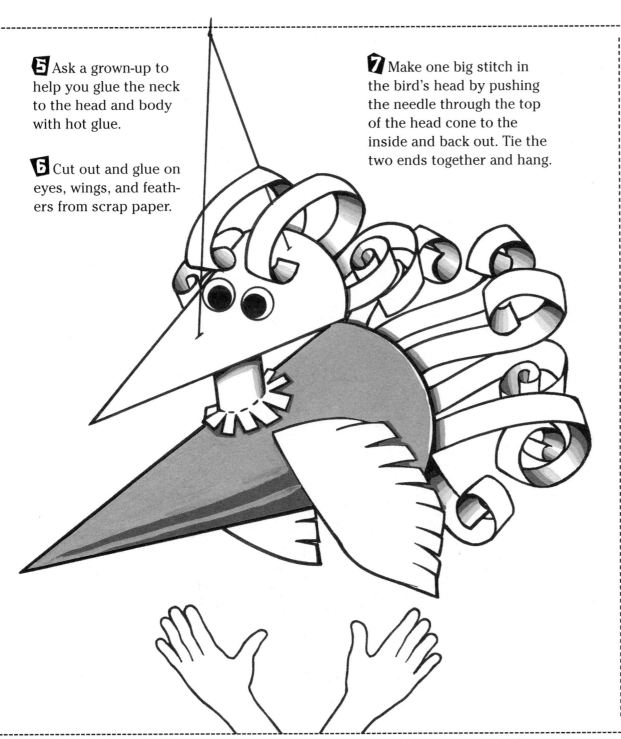

More fun!

Give a bird a helping hand in building a nest by hanging a string mesh bag filled with nesting materials outside. Fill with hair from a hairbrush, lint from the dryer, string, thread pieces, cotton balls — even dental floss! Then watch the building begin!

Check out the book *Essential Origami* by Steve and Megumi Biddle to learn how to make a folded paper crane, a classic origami design.

Level

Multicolored Butterfly

When butterflies land on flowering plants to drink sweet nectar, their feet, wings, and proboscis (strawlike sipping tube) pick up pollen and carry it to the next flower.

Here's what you need

► Construction paper scraps
► Small plastic sandwich bag
► Pipe cleaner
► Clear tape
► Monofilament or string

Here's what you do

1 Tear different colors of construction paper into dime-size pieces.

2 Fill the sandwich bag 2/3-full with paper pieces; then push extra air out of bag. Tape closed.

SANDWICH BAGS

92   **Cut-Paper Play!**

3 Divide the bag in half with the pipe cleaner to form two butterfly wings. Twist closed. Open up ends to form antennae. Hang with string.

ART OPTIONS!

◉ Twist the pipe cleaner around the middle of the filled sandwich bag several times, attaching a rubber band after the first twist. Use as a hair bow.

◉ Fill the sandwich bag with colorful cereal or pasta shapes instead of construction paper pieces.

More Fun!

👀

Make your butterfly from multicolored fabric scraps; then brush on glue over the entire figure. Let dry until fabric is stiff.

👀

Create a butterfly garden in your yard or window box by planting a variety of plants such as marigolds, dianthus, zinnias, cosmos, and milkweed.

👀

In the early summer and fall, look for the tiger-striped caterpillars of the monarch butterfly on the leaves of milkweed plants. Observe them each day for several weeks to witness the magical transformation, or metamorphosis, from caterpillar to butterfly.

Level

Slithering Snake

Young snakes shed their skin several times each year. Should you come upon a snake skin, take a moment to inspect it. Notice the different-shaped rows of scales and how long the skin is. If you take the skin home, lift it very carefully.

Here's what you need

► Construction paper
   9" x 12" (22.5 cm x 30 cm),
   any color
► Scissors
► Pencil
► Markers
► Yarn or monofilament
► Tape

Here's what you do

1 Make a point in the center of the paper. From this point, draw a spiral circle radiating outward to make the snake's body. When you get near the edge of the paper, round the line to meet the nearest line of the spiral.

2 Add eyes and designs to the snake's body with markers.

3 Cut out the snake along the spiral lines.

4 Make a mouth by tracing around the head onto the same color of construction paper. Cut out. Fold a tab along the straight edge, about 1/4" (5 mm), and glue underneath the head so the mouth is open.

5 Glue a scrap of red paper inside the mouth for a forked tongue.

6 Poke a tiny hole in the tail of the snake. Thread a piece of yarn through the hole and tape on the backside, hang; then watch your snake "slither" in the breeze!

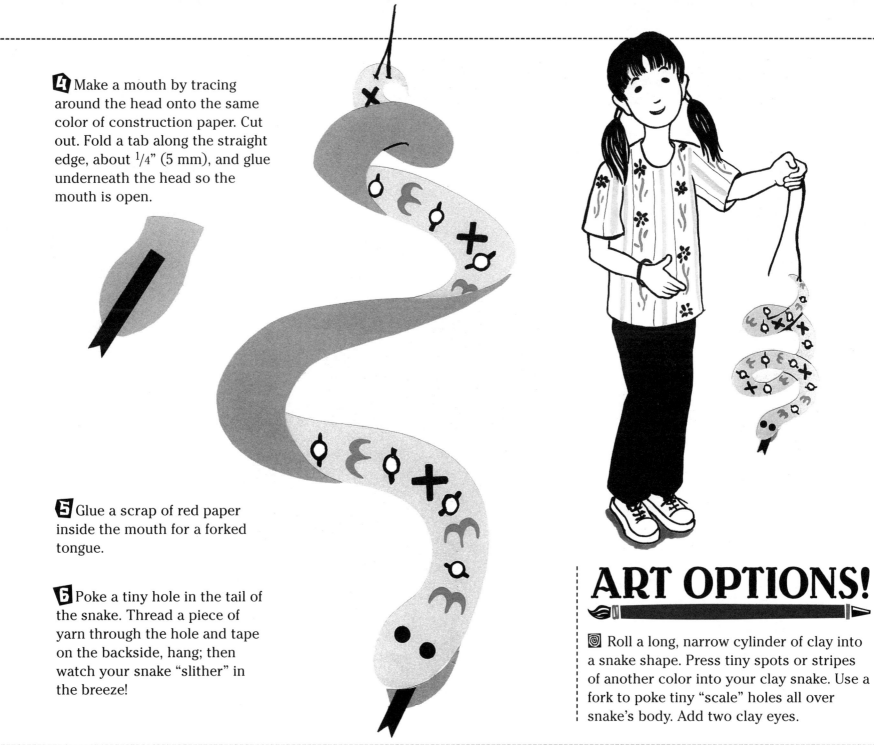

ART OPTIONS!

Roll a long, narrow cylinder of clay into a snake shape. Press tiny spots or stripes of another color into your clay snake. Use a fork to poke tiny "scale" holes all over snake's body. Add two clay eyes.

Snow People

The record for the most snowfall in a single storm occurred in Mt. Shasta, California, where 189 inches (4.8 m) fell on February 13-19, 1959! That's more than 15 feet of snow!

Here's what you need

► Construction paper, 9" x 12" (22.5 cm x 30 cm), 3 white or light color; 1 dark color
► Wide drinking glass for tracing
► Pencil
► Scissors
► Glue
► White yarn
► Markers

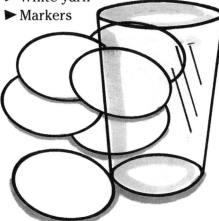

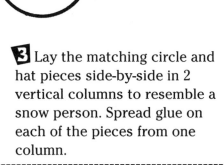

Here's what you do

1 Trace around the glass bottom 6 times onto white paper. Cut out the circles.

2 Fold the dark paper in half. Cut out a top hat and 2 boots from both halves of the folded paper for a total of 2 hats and 4 boots.

3 Lay the matching circle and hat pieces side-by-side in 2 vertical columns to resemble a snow person. Spread glue on each of the pieces from one column.

4 Place a long piece of yarn down the middle of the glue-coated pieces. Leave about 12" (30 cm) of yarn at the top to use as a hanger.

5 Sandwich the yarn with the matching pieces.

6 Glue boot pieces together; then glue to bottom circle. Glue hat pieces together; then glue to top circle.

7 Add facial features with markers.

ART OPTIONS!

◎ Make a snowflake mobile by folding paper circles (trace around a small plate) in half, then in thirds, then in half again before snipping sections from the edges of the folded paper. Create as many or as few as you wish; then sew the open snowflake "pages" together vertically with thread or monofilament before hanging.

◎ Create a snow-family mobile using a variety of sizes and colors. Then, glue on scarves from fabric scraps.

3-D Heart

The heart is a universally recognized symbol of love and friendship. Use this heart as a holiday ornament or let it be a token of your affection for someone special.

Here's what you need

► Construction paper,
    9" x 12" (22.5 cm x 30 cm),
        3 light color; 3 dark color
► Scissors
► Glue
► Yarn, 3' (90 cm) length
► Stapler

Here's what you do

1 Cut out 5 identical hearts from light-colored construction paper.

2 Stack the 5 hearts together; then glue the yarn along the center fold of the top heart, leaving the extra yarn at the top for hanging.

Cut-Paper Play!

3 Staple through all 5 hearts and yarn on the center fold. Fold over half of each heart shape so the hearts fan out and form "pages."

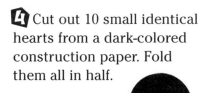

4 Cut out 10 small identical hearts from a dark-colored construction paper. Fold them all in half.

ART OPTIONS!

◎ Use this same technique to make other 3-D hanging shapes. Try using bell, star, or pumpkin shapes. Then hang several different 3-D shapes from a wire hanger.

◎ Spread glue between each fold; then sprinkle glitter onto the glue for sparkling shapes.

5 Glue the small hearts between the "pages" of the larger heart shapes.

Chinese Lantern

The Chinese end their New Year's festivities with the magnificent Lantern Festival. The occasion is celebrated to illuminate the night so people can keep watch for spirits they believe may fly across the New Year's first full moon. The Lantern Festival is one of many Chinese traditions used to usher in the New Year.

Here's what you need

► Construction paper
   12" x 18" (30 cm x 45 cm),
      1 bright color and
      1 yellow
► Ruler
► Pencil
► Scissors
► Hole punch
► Yarn
► Stapler

Here's what you do

1 Apply glue around the edges of the yellow paper; then glue to the bright-colored paper. This will make the paper stronger and give the effect of "light" inside the lantern.

2 Fold the paper in half the long way, with the yellow paper to the inside of the fold.

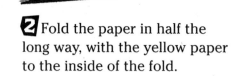

3 Place the ruler along the long edges of the paper and draw a line along the bottom edge of the ruler to serve as a guideline.

4 Place the ruler along the short edges of the paper and draw lines the width of the ruler from the fold to the guideline.

5 Cut along the vertical lines.

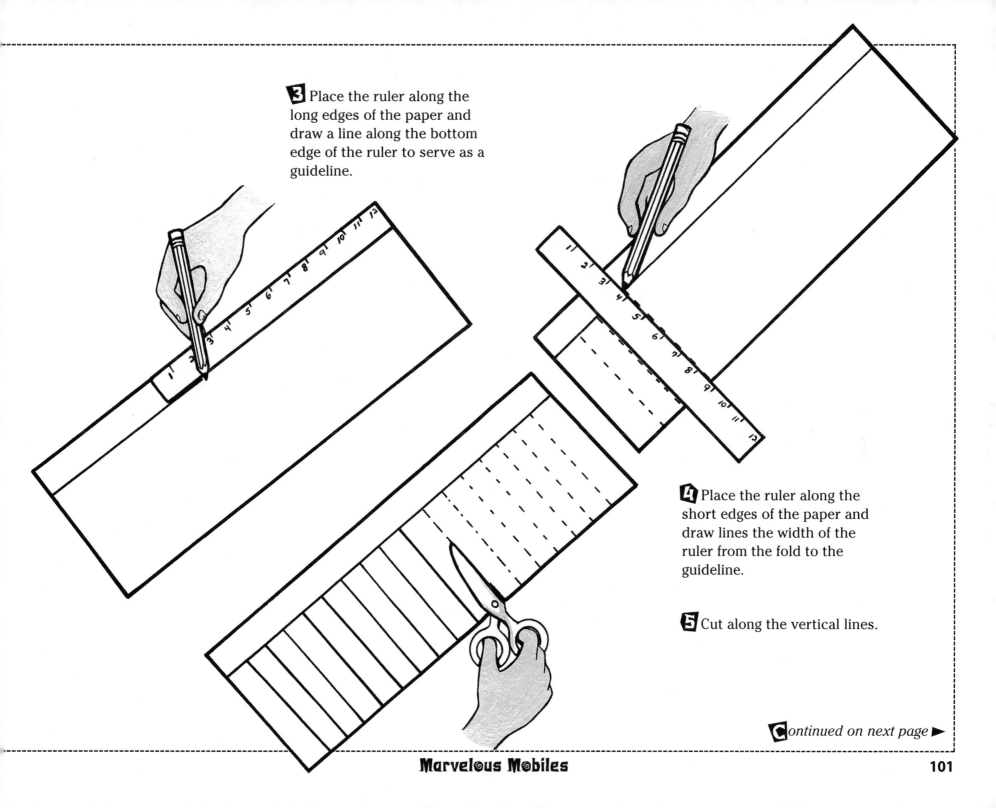

Continued on next page ▶

6 Unfold the paper and roll it into a cylinder. Staple together vertically at the top and bottom.

7 Punch 2 holes on opposite sides of the top rim of the lantern. Thread a piece of yarn through the holes and hang from the ceiling.

ART OPTIONS!

◎ Line the interior of the lantern with red cellophane or other colored cling wrap. Place a flashlight inside the lantern, dim the lights, and watch the light show!

◎ For a round lantern, fold about 1" (2.5 cm) of the top and bottom long edges of the paper. Cut vertical lines every inch or so. Roll into a cylinder shape and staple at each end.

◎ Make several different-colored lanterns and hang them on a string stretched across a room for a festive look during parties and celebrations.

Two-Dimensional Fun!

Y ou may not have known it, but you've been making two-dimensional art since you began doodling on notebook paper! Drawings, paintings, and photographs are called "two-dimensional" because they lie flat on a page without a sense of depth. Adding pizzazz to 2-D art is easier than you may think. You can create unusual backgrounds for pictures or use any number of different artistic techniques to give your art special effects.

Working with solid-color backgrounds lets you enhance, or draw attention to, your 2-D paper creations—especially if you use light and bold colors together. Using a woven background can give the effect of movement (see page 17).

Add texture to two-dimensional art by gluing on cotton, fabric pieces, buttons, or sand to your paper (see page 104). Add 3-D techniques to your 2-D art by fringing, folding, or weaving paper (see pages 15-17). Or, create unusual designs by combining one or more art techniques.

The best technique is to follow your own creative impulses in your art. Perhaps you'll want to create a cut-paper landscape with everything done in shades of a favorite color or a summer scene done only in black and white or two primary colors (see page 12). Or maybe a creation of oversized images or an entire scene done in miniature is more your style.

Using various shades of color can help you create a unique image, too (see page 111). Use bold colors to add contrast to 2-D art; imply shadows (see page 111) and texture (page 104) through different techniques.

Tricks for Texture

Adding a sense of texture to art is one way artists make their creations seem even more realistic. By using one or two simple techniques, you can show how an apple is shiny, round, and smooth or how tree bark is thick, flat, and rough. Try these tricks to get you started.

2-D Tricks

Grainy

⚙ Glue tiny paper circles (hole punch) or paper scraps close together.

⚙ Draw small dots close together. Use a combination of light and dark colors.

Rough or bumpy

⚙ Cut out small paper pieces from magazines and glue in an overlapping design.

⚙ Overlap narrow strips of paper in opposite directions. Zigzag cut or tear the edges of paper, or draw cross-hatched lines.

Smooth or soft

◉ Give shapes rounded edges.

⚙ Draw with charcoal pencil around paper edges; then smudge or blend the coal for soft edges.

3-D Tricks

Grainy

◉ Glue on sand, rice, dried oatmeal, or birdseed.

Rough or bumpy

⚙ Glue on sandpaper pieces, dried peas or beans, Velcro or fabric scraps.

Smooth or soft

◉ Glue on cotton balls, plastic wrap, or fabric scraps.

How would you show an object that's delicate? Thick? Prickly? Soft? Wet?

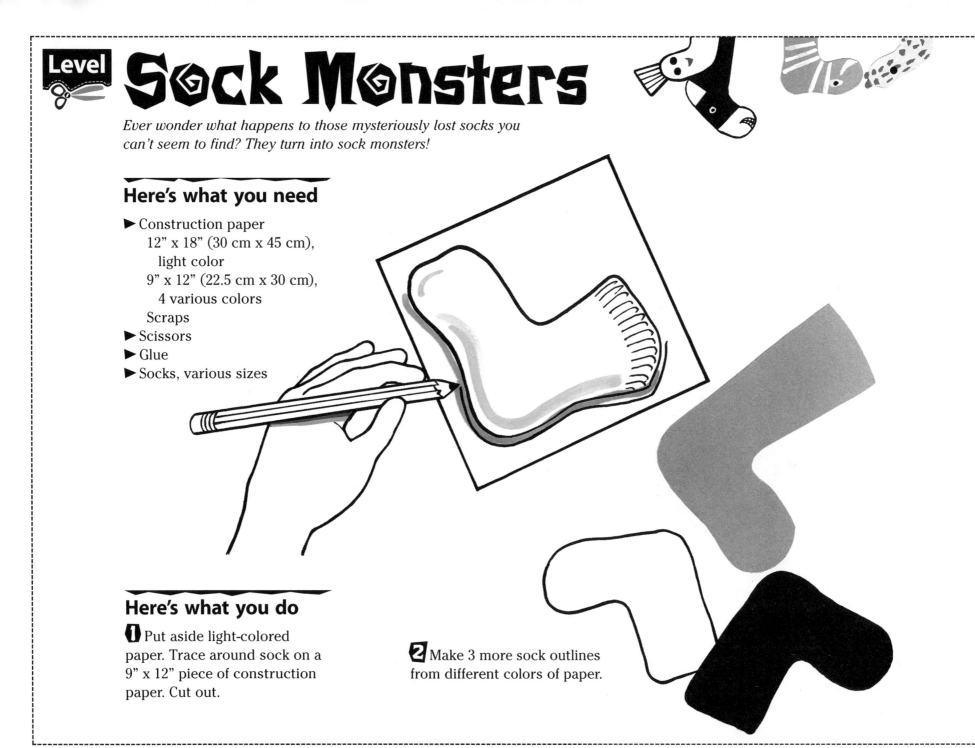

Sock Monsters

Ever wonder what happens to those mysteriously lost socks you can't seem to find? They turn into sock monsters!

Here's what you need

▶ Construction paper
   12" x 18" (30 cm x 45 cm),
      light color
   9" x 12" (22.5 cm x 30 cm),
      4 various colors
   Scraps
▶ Scissors
▶ Glue
▶ Socks, various sizes

Here's what you do

1 Put aside light-colored paper. Trace around sock on a 9" x 12" piece of construction paper. Cut out.

2 Make 3 more sock outlines from different colors of paper.

3 Arrange the shapes so one overlaps another; then glue to the light-colored paper.

4 Add personality to your sock monsters with scrap paper spots, stripes, eyes, and hair.

◎ Make a sock monster from an old sock. Stuff with another lost sock. Wrap a rubber band around the center for a head. Decorate with button eyes, felt spots, or stripes. Cut a hole for your first two fingers in both sides for puppet arms; then drape a blanket across two chairs and have a Sock Monster puppet show!

◎ Use real socks of various sizes and materials for a textured sock-monster scene.

During the mid-17th century, men's fashions were quite extravagant, with lace-trimmed shirts and hand-knitted silk stockings. Even Great Britain's King Charles I was said to have owned hundreds of pairs of handmade stockings!

Fact Find

Panamanian Paper Mola

"Mola" is a type of Panamanian folk art made by sewing together cut fabric designs for a colorful layered effect. Traditionally, mola patterns are sewn onto blouses. In fact, the word mola means "blouse" in the language spoken by the Cuna Indians. Red is the most common color used in mola design.

Here's what you need

► Construction paper
   9" x 12" (22.5 cm x 30 cm),
   1 each of black, white,
   primary, secondary, dark
   Scraps
► Scissors
► Glue

Here's what you do

1 Draw a simple outline of a bird shape or bug shape onto primary colored (such as red) construction paper. Cut out.

2 Glue the shape onto a secondary color paper, such as green. Enlarge by cutting around the entire shape, leaving about 1/4" (5 mm) of the background paper showing.

3 Glue this shape onto dark paper. Enlarge again by cutting around this shape, leaving about $1/4$" (5 mm) of dark paper showing.

4 Glue this shape onto white paper. Enlarge again by cutting around this shape, leaving about $1/4$" (5 mm) of white paper showing.

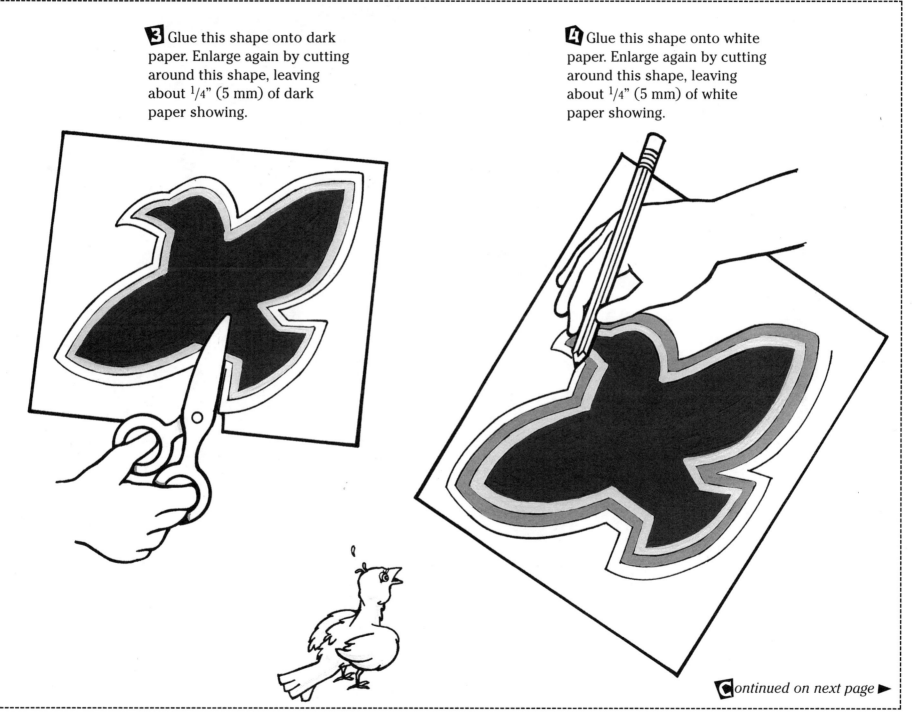

Continued on next page ▶

5 Glue your shape onto black paper.

6 Cut narrow cigar-shaped pieces in varied lengths from colored paper scraps. Glue them onto the background paper around your bug or bird shape.

ART OPTIONS!

◎ Make a "mola" design using a butterfly, flower, or animal shape.

◎ For a softer look, use colored pieces of felt. Try a combination of primary colors such as green, red, and yellow, or try a pastel-colored mola in peach, purple, and light blue.

Shady Places

Adding shades to your 2-D art will give 3-D life to whatever you're creating. Darkening one side of a shape, figure, or image will add a realistic touch to your art.

Cut-Paper Shading

1 Cut a paper strip that's a shade or two darker than the object you wish to shade.

2 Contour the shape around the outer edge of the object; then glue in place.

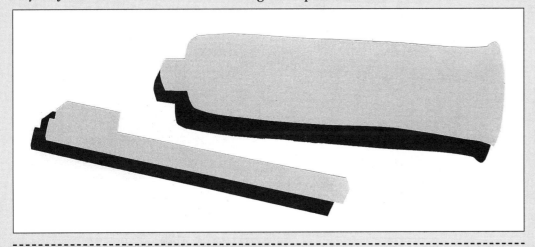

Using Charcoal

Try drawing lines at the object's edge with charcoal (found in art supply or craft stores) or soft pencil and then blending the lines for a dramatic effect. Use various grades of charcoal or different hardnesses of pencil lead for lighter and darker shades.

Drawing in Shadow

If you want to create different tones or imply shadows by drawing these effects, try cross-hatching (drawing lines that cross one another) just outside the shape or figure. Darken the area by overlapping a series of lines or by drawing tiny dots close together. For lighter tones, space the dots or cross-hatched lines farther apart.

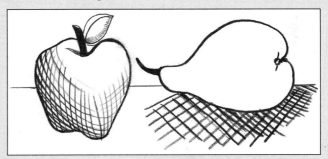

Light and dark shadows can also indicate whether an object is flat, rippled, rough, smooth, round, shiny, or dull. Use dark colors in areas that are recessed to show shadow; try light colors for shiny areas turned toward a light source (window, light, sunshine).

Cut-Paper Still Life

Still-life art often includes renderings of everyday objects such as vases of flowers and bowls of fruit. Instead of drawing a still life, try cutting the images out and gluing them to paper.

Here's what you need

► Construction paper
   12" x 18" (30 cm x 45 cm),
   black or white
   9" x 12" (22.5 cm x 30 cm),
   4 autumn colors
   Scraps
► Scissors
► Glue

Here's what you do

1 Set up a harvest still-life scene using a pumpkin, gourds, Indian corn, or any other items that remind you of autumn.

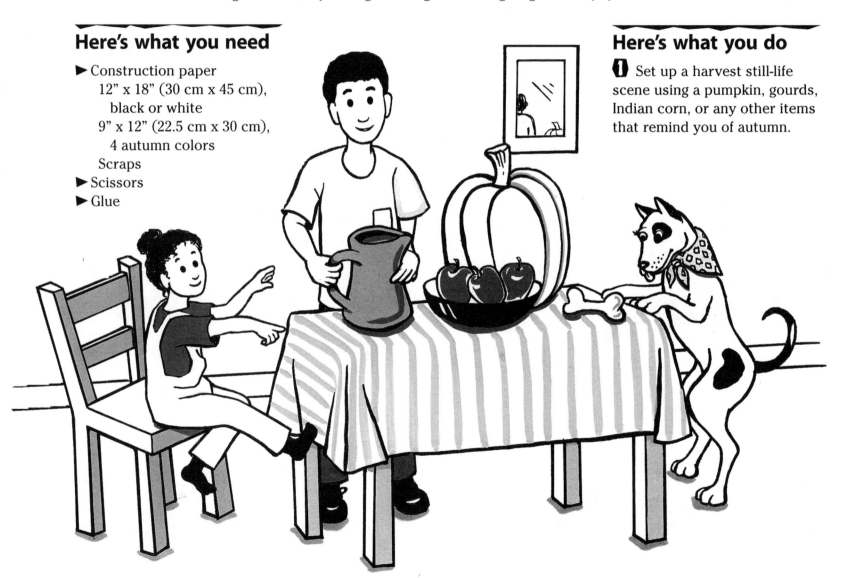

2 Choose a color paper that closely matches the object that you are representing. Cut out each shape according to how you see the objects. Let your scissors be your pencil.

3 When all the shapes are cut out, arrange and glue them on the 12" x 18" paper.

French post-impressionist painter Paul Cezanne created more than 200 still-life paintings during his lifetime (1839-1906), including many everyday objects such as fruit, dinnerware, and linens.

Fact Find

ART OPTIONS!

◎ In a still life, the artist usually wants us to see objects in a new way. Try showing the objects in your still life in an unusual position or from an unusual perspective.

◎ Try using different still-life props such as garden tools, shoes, or toys.

More fun!

👀

Paint or color a still life of everyday objects in your home. Set up a scene of a soccer ball, baseball bat, tennis racquet, and football.

👀

Visit the library and check out a book on art. Look for paintings by Cezanne, Chardin, or Picasso. What do you notice that is different about each of these artists' still-life paintings?

Robby Robot

Imagine it—your very own robot to clean your room, do your homework, or take out the trash. This paper robot is fun to make and can accomplish whatever your imagination wants it to.

Here's what you need

► Construction paper
  12" x 18" (30 cm x 45 cm),
    any color
  9" x 12" (22.5 cm x 30 cm),
    2 various colors
  Scraps
► Scissors
► Glue
► Hole punch

Here's what you do

1 Cut out 2 large squares from the 9" x 12" pieces of construction paper. Use one for the head and one for the body of your robot.

2 Cut rectangles from scrap paper for arms and legs.

3 Use paper scraps for push buttons, antennae, hand pinchers, speakers, and other robot features.

4 Assemble your robot; then glue to a piece of 12" x 18" paper.

Fact Find

ART OPTIONS!

◎ Use tin foil instead of construction paper to make a metallic robot. Decorate with markers.

◎ Create a "recycled" robot from small boxes, toilet tissue tubes, and paper tubes. Use masking tape to connect the arms and legs to the body; then glue on bolts, buttons, wire pieces, even small toy pieces.

Matisse Silhouette

Silhouettes are forms defined only by their outlines. The art of cutting silhouettes of people was popular in the late 18th and early 19th centuries, before photography was developed.

Here's what you need

► Construction paper, 12" x 18" (30 cm x 45 cm), 2 complementary colors
► Marker
► Scissors
► Friend

Here's what you do

1 Ask a friend to pose for you in an "action" pose.

2 Look at your friend, not the paper, and draw an outline of that person's shape. Do not lift the marker until the drawing is complete.

3 Cut out the drawing and glue it to the remaining sheet, marker side down.

L*ate in his life, French painter Henri Matisse stopped painting and began working with cut paper instead. He often displayed his paper cutouts on the ceiling so he could see them from bed.*

Fact Find

ART OPTIONS!

◎ Make several paper cutouts and put them together in a large mural. Add simple shapes to suggest a setting; then attach to the wall or ceiling.

◎ Matisse-style cutouts don't have to resemble people; try using the family dog, the couch, even a pile of stuffed animals as models!

More Fun!

👀

Visit a museum to see some of Matisse's wonderful paintings. Or, take out a book on Henri Matisse at the library. Look for his famous paintings *Dance* and *Red Room*. Notice the bold colors.

Smashing Silhouettes

We see silhouettes every day and every evening, too. Just look outside right now to see the silhouettes (outlines) of buildings in the distance, of mountains, and of trees against the sky. Artists have used silhouettes in their art for centuries. A silhouette portrait is usually a profile (side view), cut freehand from dark paper and mounted onto white paper for a shadow portrait.

Many paintings from Ancient Egypt show profiles of people working, playing instruments, and of animals, too. Queen Nefertiti was most often painted in profile, or side view.

⚽ Create a silhouette profile of the family pet or the car by cutting the side view or outline of the shape freehand from black paper. Glue your cut-out shape onto white paper and display your silhouette.

My Coat of Arms

Many family shields show symbols that represent characteristics deemed special by the family. A lion symbol might show courage, a rose shows beauty, or a rooster's head shows pride. Draw symbols on your coat of arms that represent the characteristics you love about your family. Or, decide what events, hobbies, sports, or interests should appear on your personal coat of arms.

Here's what you need

► Construction paper
   12" x 18" (30 cm x 45 cm),
      favorite color
   Scraps
► Scissors
► Glue
► Markers

Here's what you do

1 Fold the 12" x 18" paper in half lengthwise. Draw half of a shield shape on the fold; then cut it out. Open up the paper. If you aren't pleased with your shape, fold it and trim it a little.

2 Cut out 2 strips, about $1/2$" x 12" (1 cm x 30 cm), from black scrap paper to divide the shield in half vertically. Then, divide one of the halves into 2 sections horizontally. Trim off the excess paper.

3 Cut out your initials from paper scraps and glue them onto one small section of the shield.

4 Cut out symbols from scrap paper of something that represents your interests. Do you like flowers? Is baseball your favorite sport?

5 In the third section, represent your family, or where you live with cut outs.

More Fun!

👀

Ask members of your family about where they were born, about their parents and siblings, and where they lived growing up. Then make a family tree with all the information you've gathered to get a visual picture of your heritage.

👀

Add special effects to your coat of arms by gluing on paper quills (see page 18), fabric scraps, or old cut-up photographs.

Many governments still use shields with emblems mostly as "official seals" for state, province, and government offices. Look for shields in official photographs, on flags, or on display in government buildings.

Fact Find

Wavy Woven Mat

According to Greek legend, the Goddess Athena was so jealous of Arachne's weaving talent that she turned the young maiden into a spider (arachnid), which is why spiders weave such beautiful webs.

Here's what you need

► Construction paper
   12" x 18" (30 cm x 45 cm),
   2 contrasting colors
► Scissors
► Glue

Here's what you do

1 Fold one piece of paper in half lengthwise. Align a ruler with the top long edge of the paper and draw a line along the bottom side of the ruler.

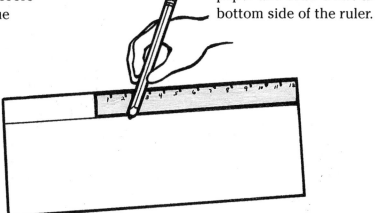

2 To make your loom, draw 5 or 6 curvy lines from the fold to the line. Cut along the lines.

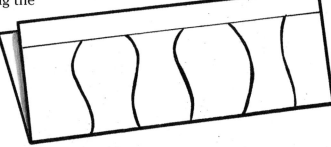

3 Open up the paper.

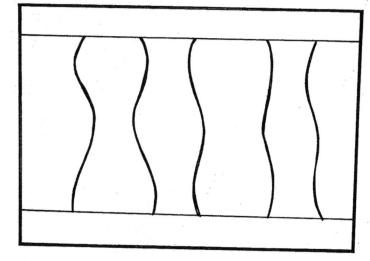

ART OPTIONS!

◎ Try using jagged lines for your loom and weaving strips for an interesting effect.

◎ Cover both sides of your woven mat with clear contact paper and use as place mats. Or, create mini woven mats for coaster squares.

4 To make weaving strips, draw 7 or 8 curvy lines across the width of the remaining piece of paper. Number the strips and cut out.

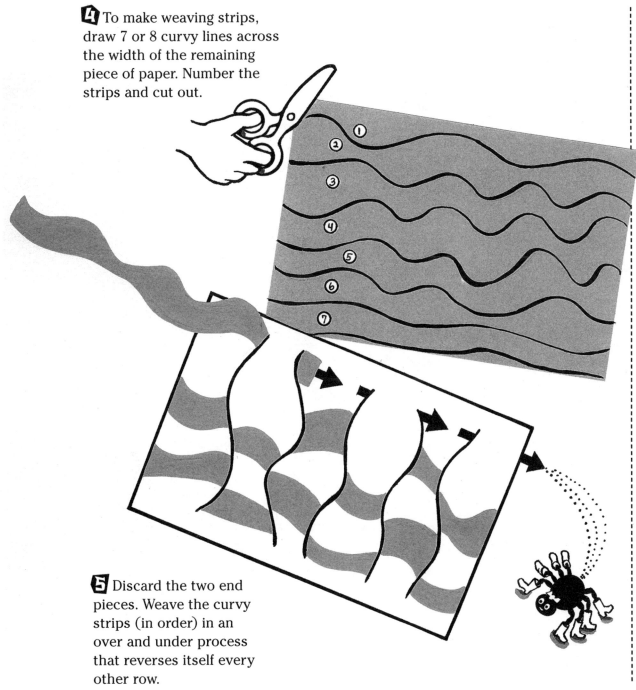

5 Discard the two end pieces. Weave the curvy strips (in order) in an over and under process that reverses itself every other row.

👀

Weave a paper box using six 1" x 9" (2.5 cm x 22.5 cm) strips, overlaid as shown. Bend the strips upwards at four corners to form sides and a square base. Weave other paper strips around through the vertical strips, from the bottom up; then fold in and glue the ends for a neat finish.

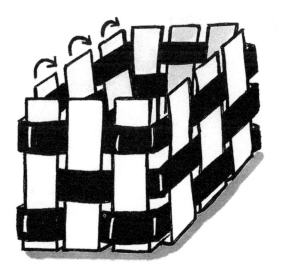

👀

What do square dancing and weaving have in common? Lots! Instead of weaving paper or wool, square dancers weave together their movements. Listen to a square dance recording; then join some friends for a do-si-do.

Clown Face

Professional clowns have their own trademark faces. Each face is a work of art designed to illustrate each clown's personality and character. You can make your own original clown face with construction paper and a little imagination.

Here's what you need

▶ Construction paper
9" x 12" (22.5 cm x 30 cm),
white and another color
Scraps
▶ Scissors
▶ Glue

Here's what you do

1 Cut a large oval out of white paper for your clown face. Glue the oval to the piece of colored background paper.

2 Make oversized smiles, frowns, eyebrows, and other exaggerated features from scraps. Glue features to the face.

3 Glue on funny paper hair (see pages 16–18 for quilling and curling) and a silly hat to the clown face.

More Fun!

Make a batch of face paint by mixing together 1 teaspoon (5 ml) cornstarch, 1/2 teaspoon (2 ml) cold cream, 1/2 teaspoon (2 ml) water, and some food coloring. Cover your face with a thin coat of cold cream and dust with baby powder for a white background. Then, use a paintbrush to apply face paint. (Use soap and water to wash it off.) Raid the closet for oversized clothes and a wig to complete your get-up!

The earliest-known clowns are thought to be the bald-headed comics of ancient Greece who performed humorous pantomime and political skits for audiences.

Fact Find

Keeping It In Proportion

Proportion is the relationship of one thing to another. Here are a few tricks for making perfectly proportioned people. They work especially well for front views of figures, but simply changing the proportions slightly will work for those seen from different angles.

Heads

⚙ Draw an oval for a head and divide into three sections by lightly drawing lines for the following three sections:

1 Top of the head to the top of the eyebrows

2 Eyebrows to bottom of the nose

3 Nose to the bottom of the chin

Facial Features

✸ Artists are masters at observing, so perk up your observation skills and check out the subtle differences in the shapes, sizes, and colors of people's facial features. To keep features proportionate, remember that the width of the nose is roughly equal to the width of one eye, and the mouth is a bit wider. Use very light lines to quickly sketch in the general locations for eyes, nose, mouth, hairline, and other features.

Bodies

✸ Mark off a body in sections, just as you did with the head. Use the size of the head to gauge one body section. A grown-up figure would be about 7 heads tall, while a child's body would be about 4–6 heads tall. Give arms about 3 heads of length and legs about 4 heads.

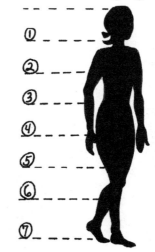

Exaggerate It!

✸ Creating something entirely unusual or unconventional is part of the fun of art. Not everything has to be in complete proportion, of course. It's the interesting differences in each of us that make us special. It's also great fun to exaggerate certain features of peoples' faces, for example. Is your smile enormous and toothy? Then exaggerate it with a giant tooth-filled grin. Look in newspapers for political cartoons with exaggerated facial features. Pretty funny, huh?

Seasonal Fun

Spring

Summer

Autumn

Winter

One of the best things about making art is you'll never need to look far for inspiration. Just peek out the window and notice the birds perched on the telephone wire, or listen to the spring peepers in a nearby lake or pond, or feel the hot desert sun. No matter where you live on earth, there's more to delight an artist than you can imagine. If you live where the trees turn yellow or red each autumn or where the cacti burst with brilliant pink blossoms in springtime, you know the inspirational power the seasons give us. What do you love most about the seasons? Get out the scissors and paper and show the world!

Level Mr. Sunshine

Many different cultures the world over have looked to the sun for artistic inspiration. In Mexico and Central America, the sun is an important theme among crafters. Let this colorful sun brighten your day.

Here's what you need

► Construction paper
   9" x 12" (22.5 cm x 30 cm),
      2 yellow; 1 orange; 1 red
   Scraps
► Salad plate for tracing
► Juice glass for tracing
► Scissors
► Glue

Here's what you do

1 Trace around the salad plate onto yellow paper and cut out.

2 Cut 7 strips each of yellow, orange, and red paper, about 1" x 4 ½" (2.5 cm x 11 cm); then cut ends at an angle to form sun rays.

3 Glue the sun rays about ½" (1 cm) from the edge around the yellow circle, alternating colors if you wish.

4 Turn over the sun.

5 To make sunglasses, trace around a small juice glass onto dark paper and cut out. Cut thin strips from the leftover black paper for side pieces and a nose piece. Glue to the sun.

ART OPTIONS!

◎ Follow steps 1–4. Then, draw a spiral line of glue from the center of the sun, radiating out to the edge of the circle. Sprinkle glitter over the glue; then shake off the excess.

◎ Create a colorful banner of the sun by cutting a large square or other shape from felt for a background. Fold down and glue the top edge to create a slot for a dowel or piece of wood. Glue on different-colored sun shapes cut from felt. Let dry; then push a dowel through the slot and hang with string from each end.

Flowers for You

In August of 1994, a group of people from Victoria, British Columbia, assembled the world's largest bouquet—10,011 roses were used to create it!

Here's what you need

► Construction paper
   9" x 12" (22.5 cm x 30 cm),
      2 of any color
   Scraps
► Scissors
► Pencil
► Glue

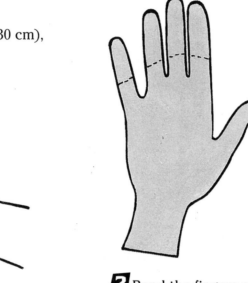

2 Bend the fingers of the paper hand as if they were grasping something.

Here's what you do

1 Trace around your hand and wrist onto one piece of paper. Cut out.

3 Glue the paper hand and wrist $2/3$ down the other piece of paper so the wrist lays off the edge a bit. Trim even with the edge of the background paper.

4 Cut 3 long, thin strips from green scrap paper for flower stems.

5 Cut 3 flowers from colorful paper and glue to the stems.

To My Special Mom
Love Johanna
xox

6 Arrange and glue stems in the palm and bent back fingers of the hand so they hold the flowers. Draw fingernails on the fingertips.

More Fun!

👀

Create a 3-D bouquet of daffodils (see page 58).

👀

Every state has its own flower associated with it. Find out your state flower; then pick a bouquet of it for the table.

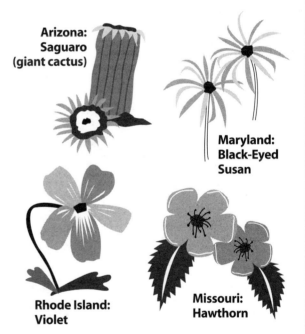

Arizona: Saguaro (giant cactus)

Maryland: Black-Eyed Susan

Rhode Island: Violet

Missouri: Hawthorn

👀

Fold a 9" x 12" piece of paper in half to make a card. Make a Flowers for You design on the front; then write a poem on the inside and give as a gift to a teacher or special friend.

Hatch-a-Chick

This oversized egg opens to reveal a happy surprise—a little paper "peeper"!

Here's what you need

▶ Construction paper
  9" x 12" (22.5 cm x 30 cm),
  white or brown
  Scraps
▶ Scissors
▶ Glue
▶ Paper fastener
▶ Markers

Here's what you do

1 Draw a large oval shape onto white or brown paper. Cut out.

2 Draw a zig-zag line like a crack across the center of the egg. Cut on line.

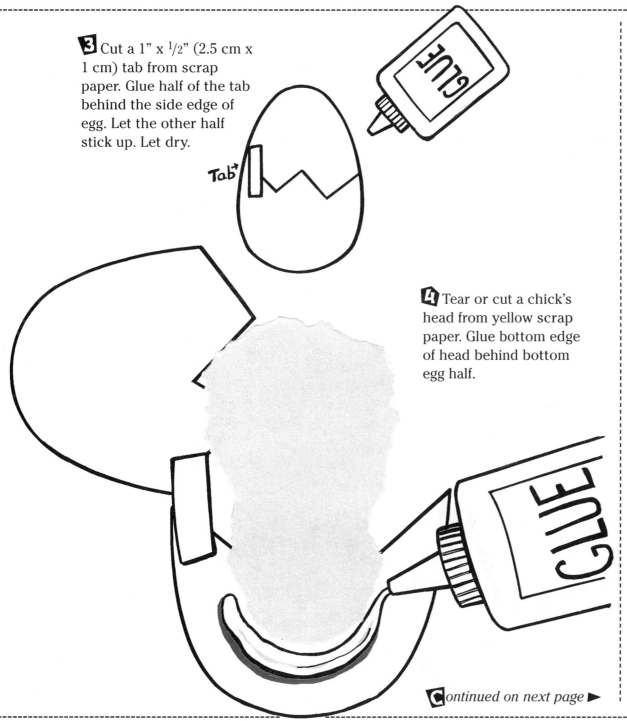

3 Cut a 1" x ¹/₂" (2.5 cm x 1 cm) tab from scrap paper. Glue half of the tab behind the side edge of egg. Let the other half stick up. Let dry.

Tab

4 Tear or cut a chick's head from yellow scrap paper. Glue bottom edge of head behind bottom egg half.

Continued on next page ▶

More fun!

👀

What other animals hatch from eggs? Take a trip to the library and find out; then put a different egg-hatching creature inside your egg.

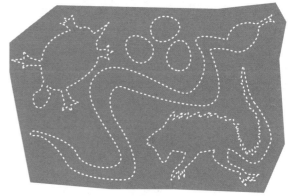

👀

Read *Jeremy Thatcher, Dragon Hatcher* by Bruce Coville.

Fact Find

*S*cientists believe the elephant bird (now extinct) of Madagascar laid the largest known bird eggs—most larger than a football! Of the world's living birds, the North African ostrich ranks as the modern layer of mammoth eggs—6 to 8 inches long (15-20 cm) and nearly 6 inches (15 cm) around!

5 Draw eyes and a beak, or cut out from scraps.

6 Fit the two egg halves together and insert a paper fastener where the top section of the egg overlaps the tab. Fold down fastener tabs and open and shut your egg.

ART OPTIONS!

◉ Make a festive egg with a colorful chick inside to welcome Easter or springtime. Use different-colored paper scraps to create a mosaic of color for the chick and the eggshell.

Sunset Silhouette

Buildings silhouetted, or outlined, against a fiery sky sunset remind us of nature's beauty within a busy city—glorious color just before dark. Homemade sunsets on paper can be just as dazzling.

Level

Here's what you need

- ► Construction paper
  - 12" x 18" (30 cm x 45 cm), yellow
  - 3" x 12" (7.5 cm x 30 cm), 6 black
- ► Orange tempera
- ► Sponge
- ► Scissors
- ► Glue

Here's what you do

1 Mix 1 tablespoon (15 ml) of orange tempera with 2 tablespoons (25 ml) of water. With a sponge, streak orange tempera across the yellow background paper. Let dry.

Continued on next page ►

2 Cut building silhouettes from black paper strips, and glue along the bottom edge of the paint-streaked paper.

3 Cut several "windows" from scrap paper, and glue to the buildings.

Dust particles, pollen, and air pollution all play a role in dramatic sunsets. As the sun sets, its light shines through these floating particles, scattering them so that only red and yellow wavelengths can be seen.

Fact Find

More fun!

Observe buildings, trees, and vehicles against the sky or horizon when the sun is setting or during a full moon. Look for the silhouettes, or outlines, of planes against the daytime sky. How many other places can you find silhouettes of objects?

Special Effects

There are a few tricks you can use to give your 2-D art creations a 3-D effect. Adding a sense of depth to your art will make them appear more realistic.

Layered Landscape

⬤ When creating a landscape, draw a horizon line about 3/4 up from the bottom edge; then think of your scene as a series of layers. Glue objects in the foreground (front) of the picture first; then midground (middle), and finally the background (back). Look outside and notice how things look in the distance. They appear smaller and higher up the farther away they are. Another easy way you can add some depth to your pictures is by overlapping shapes on the page. Objects in the foreground will overlap those in the background.

Color My World

⚙ Think about how colors look to you the farther off in the distance they are. The farther away objects are, the less vivid and bright they appear. Use lighter, softer colors for objects in the background.

Tips for Small Spaces

⚙ If your scene is confined to a smaller space, try using darker shades of color where you think holes and recesses would be in the picture and lighter colors on surfaces of objects facing any source of light.

Shining Star

Thousands of stars in a midnight sky—what a beautiful sight! Instead of waiting until nighttime to enjoy this scene, create your own.

Here's what you need

► Construction paper,
    9" x 9" (22.5 cm x 22.5 cm),
    light and dark color
► Scissors
► Hole punch
► Glue

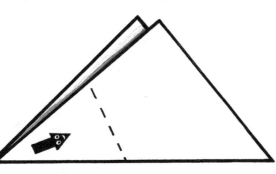

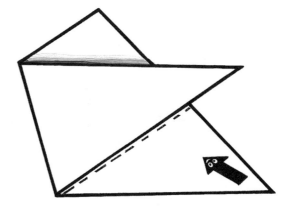

Here's what you do

1 Fold the dark-colored paper diagonally to create a triangle.

Fold one corner up across the opposite side. Repeat for the opposite corner.

Fold the shape in half again lengthwise.

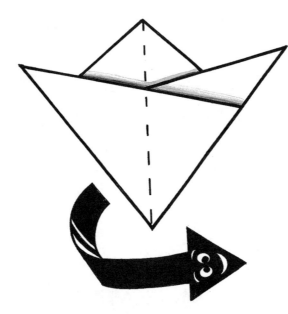

2 Cut away the bottom of the folded shape at a diagonal.

3 Unfold and flatten it out. The paper should now have a star-shaped hole in it.

4 Punch holes all over the dark paper, except near the outside edge and near the inside star hole.

5 Glue the star shape onto the light-colored paper.

◎ Add glitter to your star picture to make it sparkle.

◎ Trace around the star cutout (discarded from the project) onto white paper. Overlap the star outlines in several places. Color stars in primary colors such as red and yellow. Where stars overlap, color with a secondary color such as orange.

◎ Use the star-shaped cutout you discarded as a stencil for use on stationery, t-shirts, even borders for a bedroom (get grown-up permission first, of course!) Place the stencil on a surface and use crayons or paint to color over the exposed areas of the stencil. Try other stencil designs by folding paper in half; then cutting out a shape of your choice on the fold. Open the paper for your design.

More fun!

Many myths and legends exist about how the stars found their place in the heavens. Read *Tales of the Shimmering Sky* by Susan Milord for some of these; then make up your own tale about a star or constellation you've seen in the night sky.

Ladybug, Ladybug

Ladybugs are said to bring good luck to those who find them. In the fall, search your home—between storm windows and screens or along door cracks—for ladybugs looking for warm places to hibernate for winter.

Here's what you do

1 Trace around the bottom of the glass and the edge of the pie plate on black paper. Cut out the circles.

2 Trace around the pie plate on the red paper. Cut out.

Here's what you need

▶ Construction paper
   9" x 12" (22.5 cm x 30 cm),
   black and red
   Scraps
▶ Scissors
▶ Glue
▶ Hole punch
▶ Pie plate for tracing
▶ Drinking glass for tracing

ART OPTIONS!

🌀 Instead of gluing the wings in place, overlap the wings at the top ¹/₂" (1 cm). Insert a paper fastener so the wings will open and close.

🌀 Fringe the ends of the wings for a flying ladybug.

3 Cut the red circle in half and glue the halves to the black circle so a pie-shaped piece of black shows through.

4 Glue half of the small black circle behind the body to make a head.

5 Hole punch 30 or more black dots and glue to the red wings.

6 Hole punch 2 bright-colored circles and glue onto the head for eyes.

Ladybugs aren't true bugs, of course, they're beetles! Commonly known as the ladybird beetle, ladybugs were named in honor of the Virgin Mary, Our Lady of Beetles, during the Middle Ages.

Fact Find

Giant Sunflower

Sunflowers come in many different sizes and colors, including deep red and burgundy, orange, and gold. The tallest of these, the Paul Bunyan and Russian Mammoth, can grow as tall as 9 feet (2.8 m)!

Here's what you need

► Construction paper
   9" x 12" (22.5 cm x 30 cm),
      4 yellow; 1 brown
   1" x 12" (2.5 cm x 30 cm),
      4 green
► Scissors
► Glue
► 10" (25 cm) paper plate
► Masking tape
► Sunflower seeds
► Small bowl for tracing

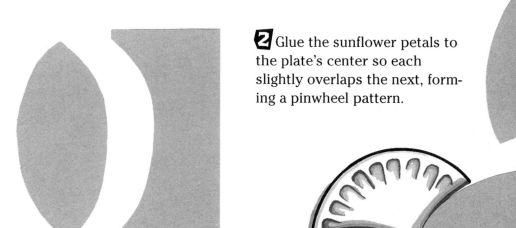

2 Glue the sunflower petals to the plate's center so each slightly overlaps the next, forming a pinwheel pattern.

Here's what you do

1 Draw, then cut out one flower petal, about 10" (25 cm) long, from yellow paper. Use the petal as a pattern; then cut out 8-10 more petals.

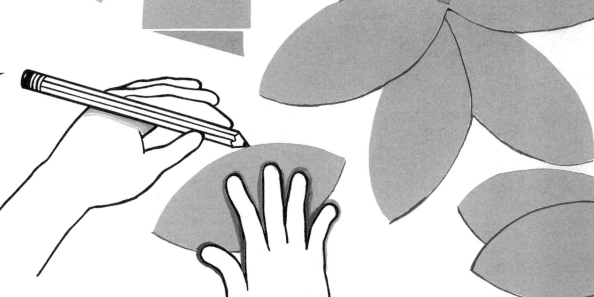

3 Trace around the rim of the bowl on brown paper. Cut out the circle and glue over the center of the pinwheel pattern.

4 Spread glue over the brown circle and sprinkle on sunflower seeds. Let dry.

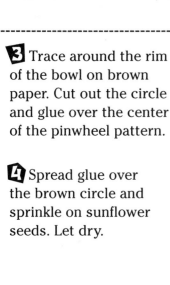

5 Glue the four green strips end-to-end for a long stem, and attach to the back of the sunflower. Use masking tape to attach to the side of the refrigerator or a door.

More fun!

Create 5 or 6 giant sunflowers grouped together on blue background or butcher paper for a lovely wall mural. Add some clouds with white chalk or cotton balls and draw a few butterflies and birds.

Save some seeds from a real sunflower in the fall to plant in a sunny place in the spring.

Shell some sunflower seeds for a nutritious snack. Add peanuts, raisins, and chocolate chips for trail mix.

Symmetrical Butterfly

If you looked closely at a butterfly, you would see that its wings are made of hundreds of tiny scales, very much like a mosaic. Make your butterfly with brilliant colors and interesting designs that are symmetrical, or the same on both sides.

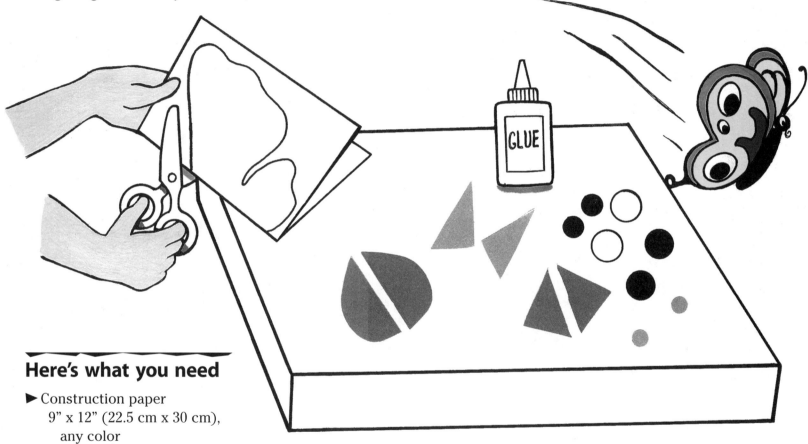

Here's what you need

► Construction paper
  9" x 12" (22.5 cm x 30 cm),
  any color
  Scraps
► Scissors
► Glue

Here's what you do

1 Fold the paper in half and draw a half-butterfly shape on the fold. Cut out and unfold.

2 Cut out interesting shapes from folded pieces of colored scrap paper. Snip each shape down the middle for 2 identical shapes.

3 Glue each shape onto each side of the butterfly so each wing is a mirror image of the other.

4 Cut a long, thin oval from dark scrap paper and glue to the center of the butterfly. Add two antennae.

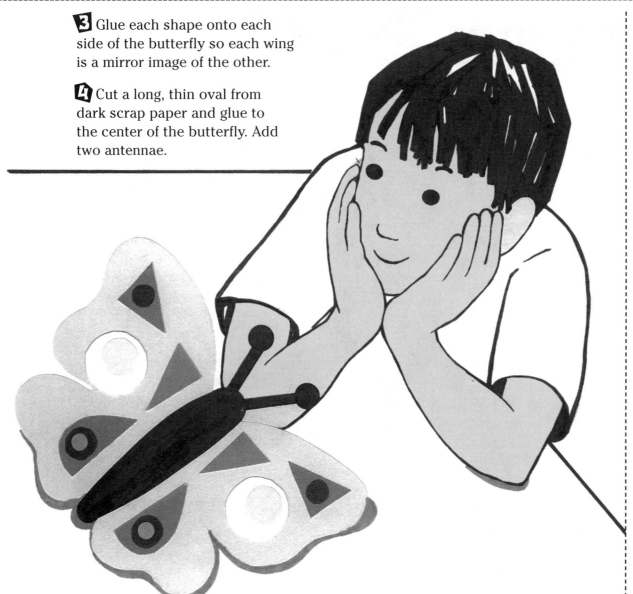

More fun!

Cut symmetrical butterfly wings out of colored construction paper. Use buttons, sequins, yarn, felt, and glitter to make a symmetrical design on the wings. Glue an oval felt piece between the wings for a body.

Visit the library and find a nature guide or book on butterflies. Look for those in your area; then go on a butterfly search and find them! How many kinds do you see?

Read a book in the library about butterflies to learn about monarchs, metamorphosis, milkweed, and how you can help the endangered monarchs.

Fact Find

The giant swallowtail is North America's largest butterfly, with a wing span of up to 6 inches (15 cm). The swallowtail is known for its slow wing beats—about 300 per minute as compared to the 450–650 per minute of other insects.

Paper Weave Fruit Basket

There is something so delicious and welcoming about a basket brimming with fruit. Weave your own special basket; then fill with cut-paper fruit shapes.

Here's what you need

► Construction paper
9" x 12" (22.5 cm x 30 cm),
any color
4" x 8" (10 cm x 20 cm),
any color
5" x 8" (12.5 cm x 20 cm),
brown
Scraps
► Scissors
► Glue
► Pencil

Here's what you do

1 Draw a line, about ¹/₂" (1 cm) from the 8" (20 cm) edge of the 4" x 8" (10 cm x 20 cm) paper.

2 Cut strips, about ¹/₂" (1 cm) wide, from the opposite edge of the paper to the line.

3 Cut 6 paper strips, about ¹/₂" x 8" (1 cm x 20 cm) from scrap paper. Weave over and under the slits in the paper. Glue the ends down.

4 Glue the woven basket to the 9" x 12" paper.

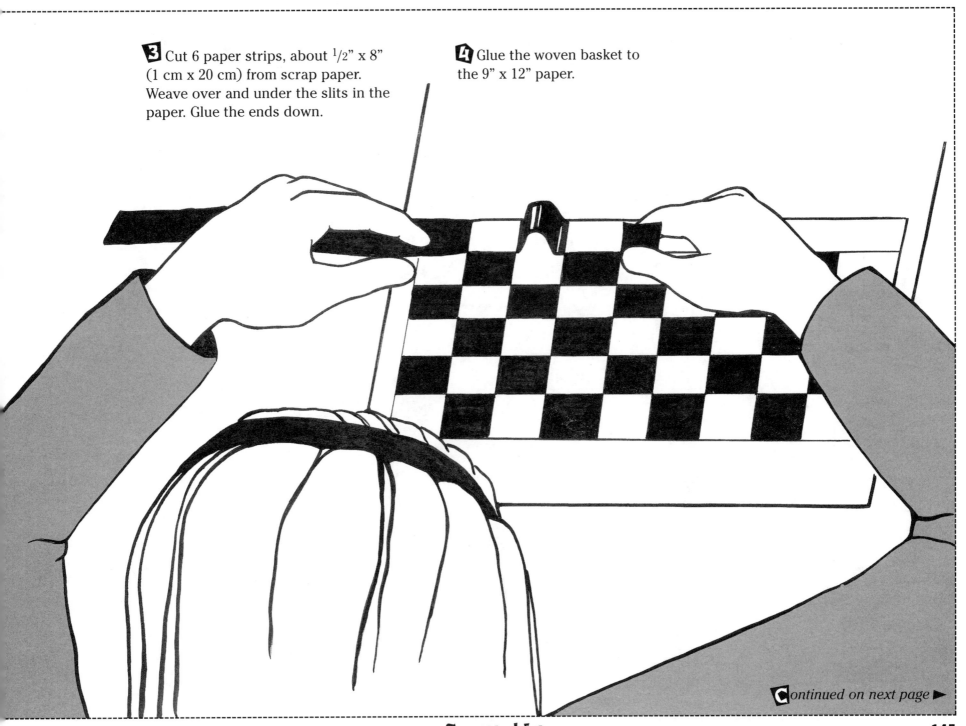

Continued on next page ▶

5 Draw an upside down U-shape on the brown paper. Cut out and glue to the basket top for a handle.

6 Cut fruit shapes from scrap paper and glue on top of the basket.

More fun!

Weave ribbon in and out of a pint-size plastic berry basket; then attach a pipe cleaner handle.

Fill a basket with tea cups, a thermos of tea, and some homemade cookies and visit an older neighbor. Compare what it was like being a child years ago and today.

Fact Find

*T*he Tohono O'odham and Hopi peoples of the American Southwest have been weaving beautiful willow baskets for hundreds of years. Today, these Native craftspeople and the Navajo use many different materials, such as cottonwood, rabbit brush, and yucca, which are often dyed, to make traditional cradleboards and intricate woven bowls.

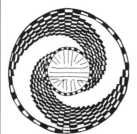

Fall Foliage

Nature gives trees a beautiful color wash during autumn! This tree gets its bright color from torn-paper leaves.

Here's what you need

▶ Construction paper
    9" x 12" (22.5 cm x 30 cm),
      blue or grey
      Scraps, autumn colors
▶ Glue

Here's what you do

1 Tear different-colored pieces of scrap paper into dime-size pieces.

2 Glue a brown strip, about 2" x 3" (5 cm x 7.5 cm), to the blue paper for a tree trunk.

3 Spread glue, a little at a time, in a large area above the trunk and on a few areas below the tree. Press the torn paper pieces onto the glue for fall foliage and falling leaves.

Continued on next page ▶

ART OPTIONS!

- Use an old magazine to find fall colors in all different places: a red dress, golden hair, or brown shoes. Cut the colors into small pieces to use for leaves; then draw a trunk and glue the paper pieces into a foliage portrait.
- Cut out a tree form and glue to light-colored paper. Cut several vertical slits in the form; then weave bright-colored paper strips, alternating colors, through the slits.

More Fun!

When the leaves have dropped from the trees, walk around and notice the "naked" tree. Are there bird or squirrel nests amid the branches? Do you notice any broken limbs? What else do you see?

Mood Indigo

Are there certain colors you like more than others? Do some colors make you feel happy? Sad? Relaxed? Excited? Well, it's no wonder, because scientists have discovered that colors really do affect our moods. If you apply this fact to art, you can give an entirely new angle to the art you create.

Artists have known for centuries the powerful effects certain colors have when they are used in their works. When they want to create a sense of warmth in their art, they use yellow, orange, and red, all considered warm colors. Green, blue, and violet are considered cool colors among artists.

Give this idea a try by creating a warm scene. What colors would you use to create a cozy, happy feeling? to represent the sun? fire? What colors would you use for a cold, wintry scene or a sense of loneliness in your picture?

 **Level**

Feathered Bird Mosaic

Hanging in the window or on the refrigerator, this mosaic bird appears ready to chirp a cheerful tune!

Here's what you need

► Construction paper
    9" x 12" (22.5 cm x 30 cm),
        bright color
    6" x 9" (15 cm x 22.5 cm),
        2 contrasting colors
    Scraps
► Scissors
► Glue

Here's what you do

1 Cut a large, rounded bird body and small head from bright-colored paper.

2 Tear many nickel-size pieces of light- and dark-colored paper. Glue alternating rows of the light- and dark-colored torn paper pieces to the bird's body and head.

Continued on next page ►

3 Cut an eye, beak, legs, feet, wings, and tail feathers from scrap paper. Glue in place.

More fun!

👀

Cut a bird's body from tagboard. Glue rows of different-colored cereal on the bird. Add details with markers.

👀

Try beating your arms as fast as a pigeon (about 3 beats per second) or a crow (2 beats per second).

👀

Read the story *Stellaluna* by Janell Cannon or *Feathers for Lunch* by Lois Ehlert.

The white-throated swift, America's fastest bird, has been clocked at speeds of up to 200 mph (330 kph). Pretty swift!

Fact Find

Penguin Figures

Birds in tuxedos? Well, not exactly, but penguins do look dressed up with their funny black and white feathers.

Here's what you need

► Construction paper
  12" x 18" (30 cm x 45 cm), white
  9" x 12" (22.5 cm x 30 cm), 2 black; 1 white
  6" x 6" (15 cm x 15 cm), light color
► Scissors
► Glue
► Pencil

Here's what you do

1 Draw and cut out 4 penguin shapes (imagine a plump bowling pin) from black paper. Position them on the 12" x 18" white paper in the direction you want them to face.

2 Using a scrap of leftover black paper, cut out wings. Use white paper for bellies and eyes. Cut out beaks and feet from the light-colored scrap paper.

3 Glue all parts in place.

Mosaic Snow Person

Mosaics date back to around 3000 B.C., where they were used in making decorative floor designs in the Near East. Many materials, such as pebbles, glass, clay—and paper!—make wonderful mosaics.

Here's what you need

► Construction paper
   9" x 12" (22.5 cm x 30 cm),
      1 white and 1 dark color
   Scraps
► Glue
► Scissors
► Hole punch

Here's what you do

1 Tear away the straight edges from the white paper; then tear the paper into dime-size pieces.

2 Draw 3 overlapping circles on the dark-colored paper for a snow person.

The oldest mosaics known were found in pavement made thousands of years ago in Greece, Turkey, and the island of Crete. Colored pebbles were laid together in a cementlike mixture to create these beautiful walkways.

Fact Find

3 Spread glue evenly over one circle at a time; then press the torn pieces of white paper onto the glued areas, covering them completely.

4 Cut out eyes, mouth, and buttons from scrap paper, using a hole punch. Cut out hat, nose, and stick arms from scrap paper. Glue in place.

ART OPTIONS!

◎ Create mosaic decoupage by cutting a variety of colored papers into squares, triangles, and circles. Use a hole punch for circles and cut squares from strips of paper. Glue the pieces in a design to cover a small jewelry box, a paper plate, or a light switch cover.

More fun!

Make an icy snow cone treat by placing 1 cup (250 ml) of clean snow in a paper cup. Pour grape or other favorite juice over the snow; then slurp it up!

Poinsettia

Make your own paper poinsettia for holiday decorations or to brighten up winter days.

Here's what you need

▶ Construction paper
   3" x 6" (7.5 cm x 15 cm),
      7 red; 7 green
   Scraps
▶ Scissors
▶ Glue

Here's what you do

1 Fold each piece of red and green paper lengthwise. Beginning at one end and ending at the other, cut a half oval shape from each piece of paper. Do not cut on the fold.

The red "petals" of the poinsettia aren't really petals at all. Native to Mexico, the poinsettia has bright red leaves called bracts and green foliage. The flowery part of the poinsettia are the tiny yellow flowers found at the center of the plant.

Fact Find

2 Cut out a 4" (10 cm) circle from green scrap paper.

3 Put a dot in the center of the green circle and glue the 7 red petals from the center dot in a pinwheel pattern.

4 Glue the green petals behind the green circle so they show between the red petals.

5 Crumple several nickel-sized pieces of yellow scrap paper into little balls. Glue in the center of the poinsettia.

ART OPTIONS!

◎ Create a 3-D poinsettia mobile by making 2 identical shapes. Slit one shape up from the bottom and the other shape down from the top. Slide the two shapes together and hang.

◎ Create a beautiful poinsettia wreath. Make 8 poinsettias and tape in a circle on a wall, the refrigerator, or a wreath-shaped piece of tagboard.

◎ Instead of crumpling yellow paper for the center, use yellow hole punch circles. Glue the poinsettia onto colored paper and cover with contact paper for a festive place mat.

More fun!

The bracts of the poinsettia stay red for many weeks, but once they turn green, don't throw away the plant. Instead, prune back the leaves and put outside for the warm weather. Water well and in the fall (before the cold sets in) bring the plant inside to a room or closet that is dark 12 hours each day. When the plant begins to show color again, bring it out to enjoy.

Activities by Level of Challenge

Guide to Art Techniques

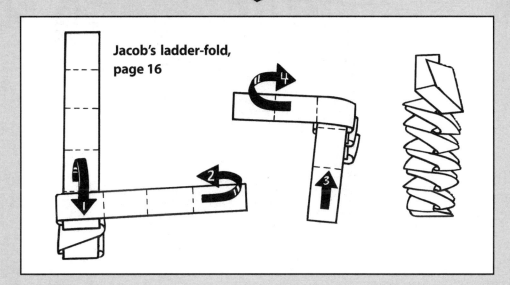

Jacob's ladder-fold, page 16

More Good Books from Williamson Publishing

Kids Can!®

The following *Kids Can!*® books for ages 4 to 10 are each 160-178 pages, fully illustrated, trade paper, 11 x 8 ¹/₂, $12.95 US. To order additional copies of *CUT-PAPER PLAY!* or any of these books, please see last page. Thank you.

VROOM! VROOM!
Making 'dozers, 'copters, trucks & more
by Judy Press

COOL CRAFTS & AWESOME ART!
A Kids' Treasure Trove of Fabulous Fun
by Roberta Gould

HAND-PRINT ANIMAL ART
by Carolyn Carreiro

SUPER SCIENCE CONCOCTIONS
50 Mysterious Mixtures for Fabulous Fun
by Jill Frankel Hauser

Parents' Choice Gold Award Winner
Parents Magazine Parents' Pick
THE KIDS' NATURE BOOK
365 Indoor/Outdoor Activities and Experiences
by Susan Milord

KIDS' COMPUTER CREATIONS
Using Your Computer for Art & Craft Fun
by Carol Sabbeth

Benjamin Franklin Best Multicultural Book Award Winner
Parents' Choice Approved
Skipping Stones Multicultural Honor Award Winner
THE KIDS' MULTICULTURAL COOKBOOK
Food & Fun Around the World
by Deanna F. Cook

Parents' Choice Approved
Dr. Toy Vacation Favorites Award Winner
KIDS GARDEN!
The Anytime, Anyplace Guide to Sowing & Growing Fun
by Avery Hart and Paul Mantell

Winner of the Oppenheim Toy Portfolio Best Book Award
American Bookseller Pick of the Lists
THE KIDS' SCIENCE BOOK
Creative Experiences for Hands-On Fun
by Robert Hirschfeld and Nancy White

Parents' Choice Gold Award Winner
American Bookseller Pick of the Lists
Winner of the Oppenheim Toy Portfolio Best Book Award
THE KIDS' MULTICULTURAL ART BOOK
Art & Craft Experiences from Around the World
by Alexandra M. Terzian

Parents' Choice Gold Award Winner
Benjamin Franklin Best Juvenile Nonfiction Award Winner
KIDS MAKE MUSIC!
Clapping and Tapping from Bach to Rock
by Avery Hart and Paul Mantell

Other Books from Williamson Publishing